Five Bodies

Theory, Culture & Society

Theory, Culture & Society caters for the resurgence of interest in culture within contemporary social science and the humanities. Building on the heritage of classical social theory, the book series examines ways in which this tradition has been reshaped by a new generation of theorists. It also publishes theoretically informed analyses of everyday life, popular culture, and new intellectual movements.

EDITOR: Mike Featherstone, *Nottingham Trent University*

SERIES EDITORIAL BOARD
Roy Boyne, *University of Durham*
Mike Hepworth, *University of Aberdeen*
Scott Lash, *Goldsmiths College, University of London*
Roland Robertson, *University of Aberdeen*
Bryan S. Turner, *University of Cambridge*

THE TCS CENTRE
The Theory, Culture & Society book series, the journals *Theory, Culture & Society* and *Body & Society*, and related conference, seminar and postgraduate programmes operate from the TCS Centre at Nottingham Trent University. For further details of the TCS Centre's activities please contact:

Centre Administrator
The TCS Centre, Room 175
Faculty of Humanities
Nottingham Trent University
Clifton Lane, Nottingham, NG11 8NS, UK
e-mail: tcs@ntu.a.uk
web: http://tcs.ntu.ac.uk

Recent volumes include:

Critique of Information
Scott Lash

Liberal Democracy 3.0
Stephen P. Turner

French Social Theory
Mike Gane

Thorstein Veblen on Culture and Society
Stjepan Mestrovic

Five Bodies

Re-figuring Relationships

John O'Neill

SAGE Publications
London • Thousand Oaks • New Delhi

SAGE Publications Ltd
1 Olivers' Yard
55 City Road
London EC1Y 1SP

SAGE Publications Inc
2455 Teller Road
Thousand Oaks, California 91320

SAGE Publications India Pvt Ltd
B-42, Panchsheel Enclave
Post Box 4109
New Delhi 100 017

British Library Cataloguing in Publication data

A catalogue record for this book is
available from the British Library

ISBN 0 7619 4308 0
   0 7616 4309 9

Library of Congress control number available

Typeset by C&M Digital (P) Ltd., Chennai, India
Printed and bound in Great Britain by Athenaeum Press, Gateshead

Marius and Joan

Contents

List of Figures

Preface

In the 1980s I put forward a framework for a sociology of the body – a field which did not have a name when I started lectures on it after my first book, *Sociology as a Skin Trade* (1972). The exponential growth of body studies meantime obliged one to take a stand. I did so by making a forthright statement on the body as an *institution of anthropomorphosis*. In *Five Bodies* those cultural practices through which we map our macro–micro worlds, articulating a cosmology, a body politic, a commensal society, a productive/consumptive economy and a bio-technological frontier of human design and transplantation are focused upon.

My argument proceeds in terms of a civilizing thesis drawn from Vico's humanist *The New Science* ([1774] 1970) and Freud's melancholic reflections on the figure of prosthetic 'man' in *Civilization and its Discontents* (1962). The immediate context of my own body studies was the body politics of the 1960s experienced from the Canadian border of North America. Here events appeared both to challenge and to celebrate the social sciences that we were revisioning through continental phenomenology, hermeneutics and critical theory (O'Neill, 1974; 1989). At the same time I thought it necessary to preserve the grand perspectives of the classical order problem – moving from cosmological societies to Judeo-Christian society, into the industrialized orders of work, consumption, life and death that characterize modernity and its aftermath (Turner, 1984; Shilling, 1993).

Five Bodies avoids any essentialist position on the logic of the body in favor of the open body-logics that are captured in the history of 'anthropomorphism' or of becoming-human. It never loses sight of the interaction between our ways of thinking bodies through society and thinking/doing society through bodies (O'Neill, 2002a). It therefore never privileges patriarchal, feminist or racialized body-logics that have been the focus of later research. Rather, I show how corporeal practices, such as the ritual meal, can be thought of in terms of contested theories of functionalism and materialism obliging one to locate oneself as theorist. Or I show how archaic cosmology is in fact an elaborate cognitive mapping practice which remains a civilizing source as we explore futuristic inner and outer worlds. *Five Bodies* is also concerned with issues of sovereignty and kinship, emancipation and alienation. Between the 1960s and the 1970s we moved from idealizing our bodies to being horrified by them as our sense of the sources of empowerment shifted. I have therefore argued for the institution of a civic ratio between public and private life, work, health and education which demand our collective and familied intelligence. Here, especially, I call for a civic resistance to the marketization and reductive medicalizing of the welfare state rather than its dismissal as a uniquely disciplinary complex, as argued by Foucault (O'Neill, 1995). The issues here have become ever more urgent since the 1980s and 1990s with the development of the bio-state/market complex with which I close the book but not the continuing argument which will likely refigure all our relationships.

We may distinguish four dimensions or phases of the contemporary articulation of the life sciences and the refigured body politic that derives from each knowledge-base (Gilbert, 1995: 571):

1 the neural body (text) and politics as culture/law (context);
2 the genetic body (text) and politics of ethnicity/race (context);
3 the immune body (text) and agonistic politics (context);
4 the phenotypic body (text) and embodied politics (context).

We shall see in Chapter 3, on the body politic that it is the neural body that is a model of hierarchical, male-brain society – with its potential for patriarchal sexism and racism. It is also the model for 'Encyclopedic Man' (Figure 1.1). The neural body had to learn to adapt its monarchical bias to a constitutional state. This shift becomes more pronounced with the discovery of the immune body/self, the agent of political conflict, defending itself from outside attacks or infections. The neural and immune body selves both suffered severe setbacks with the discovery that the mind and the body could attack themselves – as with cancer, Alzheimer's disease and AIDS. Finally, the genetic body forms by replication rather than learning and socialization. It is the biological constant of selfhood. The neural immune and genetic bodies are wrapped, so to speak, in the phenotypic or incarnate body of corporate life. This is the body that irrupts from time to time to resist the hardening and antagonisms of class, race and gender politics.

I hope to have cut into the issues in a way that preserves the humanist ideal of making our place in a civic cosmos. Here we do not rule out contingency and conflict but constitute a civic arena in which we engage contested ideas and practices. My perspective on embodied society is achieved through an historical and structural approach characteristic of classical studies, anthropology and Hegelian/Marxist sociology (O'Neill, 1982c; 1996).

This obliges me to look for fine detail for its own sake and then to find a larger picture/puzzle for our own sake! When I am concerned with detail (or data), it is in the first place out of respect for the phenomenological canniness of even the most uncanny practices. So I do not mean to overwhelm these observations in postmodern critical irony (O'Neill, 1995). When I am concerned with theory (*theoria*), I mean to respect thought's desire for formality, i.e., its wish to think its observations so as to constitute good enough sociology, with a little help from other social sciences similarly constituted.

Today, any reader in cultural studies will already have absorbed a considerable culture of body science and body folklore. The exponential take-off in our body culture within which we may locate cultural studies of every kind of bodily practice guarantees that the present offering can only hope to strike a chord here and there with those who still work towards a future that exceeds the grasp of our greedy present.

Introduction

The Prosthetic God

We love to wear machines – anything from sunglasses to a cigar, from a watch to a car. We even love to carry machines – anything will do, from walking stick to a boombox, from the *Portable Nietzsche* to a mobile (phone). We hate to switch off our engines. Lest we switch off ourselves, we leave our motors running, the lights on, the radio in the background, the TV over the bar, the refrigerator, or the humidifier. When we die, there has to be someone willing to switch off the machines that otherwise persist in living for us. We look good to ourselves in machines: they are the natural extensions of our narcissistic selves. They magnify us, and at the same time amplify the world we have chosen to create for ourselves – the 'man-made' world. There is no escaping our romance with the machine we have created in order to recreate ourselves. Nothing praises our divinity like our machines; nothing else renders us at once more powerful and more fragile. No holocaust is greater than the one we consecrate to our machines built to destroy as much in peace as in war and which we never cease to improve for either end.

As prosthetic gods, we lack any perspective on the divinity of our machines. The more they kill us, the more we turn to them for safety; the more they sicken us, the more we turn to them for health; the more they cripple us, the more we turn to them for repairs. What it is important to see is that in every case our power over nature – or our power over life – is a power over ourselves (*biotext*) inscribed through the state and the economy, and through its laws and sciences (*sociotext*). As I see it, then, all of these disciplinary strategies of power may be thought of as biotechnologies. This move is intended as a deconstructive strategy – a deliberate 'misreading', if you will – whose aim is to bring biotechnology as a series of specific biological and medical engineering practices within the realm of the biopolitical. Thus, we are concerned with how it is that in modern society we are devising a technology for rewriting the genetic code much as savage societies once rewrote the flesh – but in a different key, played first upon the body of desire:

> For capitalism is the stage in which all the excitations, all the pleasures and pains produced on the surface of life are inscribed, recorded, fixed, coded in the transcendent body of capital. Every pain costs something, every girl at the bar, every day off, every hangover, every pregnancy; and every pleasure is worth

something. The abstract and universal body of capital fixes and codes every excitation. They are no longer, as in the bush, inscribed in the bare surface of the earth. Each subjective moment takes place as a momentary and singular pleasure and pain recorded on the vast body of capital circulating its inner fluxes, ... in short, there is ... a going beyond the primary process libido to the organization man. The dissolute, disintegrated savage condition, with the perverse and monstrous extension of an erotogenic surface, pursuing its surface affects, over a closed and inert, sterile body without organs, one with the earth itself – this condition is overcome, by the emergence of, the dominion of, the natural and the functional. The same body, the working body, free, sovereign, poised, whose proportion, equilibrium and ease are such that it dominates the landscape and commands itself at each moment. Mercury, Juno, Olympic ideal. (Lingis, 1978: 101–2)

When he stood back to contemplate our civilization and its discontents, Freud could not envisage the new bioprosthetics that would once again open the civilizational frontier, creating new powers and new dependencies in us. Humankind has wrapped itself in a science and technology whose omnipotence has delivered us from our childhood into a certain if uncomfortable divinity: 'Man has, as it were, become a kind of prosthetic god. When he puts on all his auxiliary organs he is truly magnificent; but these organs have not grown on him and they still give him trouble at times' (Freud, 1962: 38–9).

In the following chapters, I stand at some distance from Freud's conception of the infantile nature of the first humans and their gods, and so I am less inclined to abuse them with the faults of our modern technological fixation. Rather, I am concerned to rethink the civic legacy bequeathed to us in the *sociopoetics* of the first humans whose families and gods have survived most of the history of our own inhumanity and are still alive in the most ordinary places of mankind. If we have anything to fear from humanity's capacity for metamorphosis, it is from the awful potential we now have to erase all other living forms along with ourselves. The truly unthinkable side of our civilizational discontent is that we may well be the first human society to think of itself as the *last*. Before such a prospect, we are obliged to rethink the human body to reconstitute its family, its political economy and its biotechnologies. Such a task cannot be indifferent to us, as the continuing protests from the young men and women of the world testify. If the old men who command greed and destruction do not awaken from their extraterrestrial fantasies, we shall not be lucky enough even to leave behind us any marked grave and certainly no child of our civilization, nor any gods.

Our Two Bodies

Anthropomorphism. Attribution of human form or character.

a. Ascription of a human form and attributes to the Deity.
b. Ascription of a human attribute or personality to anything impersonal or irrational.

(*Oxford English Dictionary*)

Despite the dictionary, I propose that human beings cannot do without the practice of anthropomorphism. If they were to refrain from it entirely, the world would assume a character more alien than that of any deity. Therefore anthropomorphism is an essential human response; it is a creative force in the civic shaping of human beings and of their civil and divine institutions. It is a conceit of logicians that we could think otherwise. Yet, how dare I reinvent anthropomorphism? Even if I am not afraid of fallacy, oughtn't I to respect intellectual fashion? We do not belong in our own creation – any more than God. This may seem odd but, so we are told, it is better looked upon as an exciting opportunity – supposing we survive the invitation to social and moral chaos. We do, more or less. But I think we survive by living off borrowed moral capital. Therefore I want to raise the old question: who makes us? This is the anthropomorphic question. By asking it and in looking for responses to it, we make ourselves human.

It is essential for us to proceed in this way. We cannot otherwise establish the radical grounds of an anthropomorphizing social science. The loss of the human in the social and literary sciences meets with equal lament and celebration. The progress of human knowledge seems to require the abandonment of an anthropocentric or human-centered world-view – a proposition I do not seriously challenge. It has become clear, however, that in the process people have lost the power to give a civic shape to human institutions, which I think we must revive if we are to defend ourselves against the equal excesses of subjective and subjectless science. Moreover, I believe that the vital issues in the complex civic relation between persons, nature, and social institutions may well be approached through our unavoidable interest in the human body. We shall see in some detail how the human body is an intelligent and critical resource in the civic production of those small and larger orders that underlie our social, political, and economic institutions. Such an argument is at first sight far from obvious, since the body is generally regarded as something either far too intimate or else far too unruly to be the starting place for a study of the intelligent order in our public lives. It seems odd, for example, to speak of a *sociology* or of a *political economy of the body*. The body would surely seem to lie outside the concerns of sociology, economics, and politics as these disciplines are generally understood. But to the extent this is so, much of what we ordinarily know and feel about our lives and the quality of our public life is ignored.

In what sense do we understand the body that enters into our social life? It is sometimes thought that the body is a physical object like other objects that surround us. As such, our *physical body* can be bumped into, knocked over, crushed, and destroyed. Yet, even as we say this, our language is estranged or alienated from the *lived body*, that is, that communicative bodily presence to which we cannot be indifferent, to which we are as sensible in others as in ourselves (O'Neill, 1989). Because of the inseparability of these two bodies, we treat even the physical body as a *moral body* to which we owe respect, help, and care, and for whose injuries we are responsible even in our own person. Moreover, civic society strongly sanctions the protection of bodies. Those who inflict deliberate injury upon others risk incarceration and other bodily harms, and even those who are merely clumsy risk at least embarrassment, if not moral condemnation. Thus, even the physical body is, morally speaking, more than a simple object for biological study or medical practice and may in fact require us to rethink their procedures: witness the reinvention of holistic medicine. In any case, we cannot treat the anatomy and physiology of the body as paradigmatic of what persons are required to know about bodily conduct and comportment in social settings. The *communicative body* we learn to think and have is the general medium of our world, of its history, culture, and political economy.

> The body is our general medium for having a world. Sometimes it is restricted to the actions necessary for the conservation of life, and accordingly it posits around us a biological world; at other times, elaborating upon these primary actions and moving from their literal to a figurative meaning, it manifests through them a core of new significance: this is true of motor habits such as dancing. Sometimes, finally the meaning aimed at cannot be achieved by the body's natural means; it must then build itself an instrument, and it projects thereby around itself a cultural world. (Merleau-Ponty, 1962: 146)

The preceding distinctions are not meant to diminish the importance in our lives of the biological body. I mean only to deepen the connections between biology and civic culture which arise precisely because the human body is a communicative body whose upright posture and audiovisual articulation open up a symbolic world that enriches our experience beyond any other form of life (Grene, 1965). We never experience those aspects of the body I have differentiated as the physical body and the communicative body except as a unity comprising incredible variety, depending on historical and social circumstances. Societies have come to no universal agreements about the proper ritualization of the bodily experiences of birth, death, pain, pleasure, hunger, fear, beauty, and ugliness. How, then, are we to regard the body as a topic of inquiry for social science rather than as the object solely of biomedical science? What is to be learned about the body that could possibly aid us in our understanding of the larger issues of social order, conflict, and change? Even if there were anything to be learned, how would it be of more than passing interest? Surely science is in pursuit of order, regularity and generalizations that are independent of bodily behavior? Generally speaking, sociology is the study of the rules and normative behavior that proceed from people's beliefs and not from their bodily chemistry or physiology. Therefore, it will be said, *society is in our minds, not in our bodies*. Such, at any rate, might be concluded from centuries of religious, philosophical, and educational practice. We conceive of public order dualistically, that is to say as the rule of mind over matter, or of reason over the senses. In this view our bodies are the unwilling servants of the moral and intellectual order. Thus we need to discipline our bodies to achieve excellence, to enter heaven, or to endure the passivity of sitting in a lecture hall to gather the good news of sociology, let alone to read this book!

It is not an easy task to understand how social institutions rethink the body (Mauss, 1973). It is even more difficult to understand how *we can rethink institutions with our bodies*. But this is what we shall be doing in this book. Michel Foucault has brought to our attention the difficult notion that, far from repressing the body, modern political economy exercises power over it by opening up, so to speak, the sexual body as a discursive channel into which we confess endlessly who we are and what we desire:

> Sexuality must not be described as a stubborn drive, by nature alien and of necessity disobedient to a power which exhausts itself trying to subdue it and often fails to control it entirely. It appears rather as an especially dense transfer point for relations of power: between men and women, young people and old people, parents and offspring, teachers and students, priests and laity, an administration and a population. Sexuality is not the most intractable element in power relations, but rather one of those endowed with the greatest instrumentality: useful for the greatest number of maneuvers and capable of serving as a point of support, as a linchpin, for the most varied strategies. (Foucault, 1980: 103)

I think it is necessary to keep in mind that the reduction of the communicative body to the sexual body is a historical process that distorts the gendered cosmology that governed nature, society and the human body subordinating it to the industrialization of nature and the human family (Illich, 1982), which we shall discuss in later chapters. Thus I have reconstructed this history in terms of what I call the shift from history as *biotext* to history as *sociotext* (see the Conclusion), and this provides the frame upon which the following chapters hang. At the same time, I wish to take a radical stand against antihumanism and, in particular, against any fashionable credo of *defamilization*, whose aim is to strengthen the market as the ultimate matrix of human life. I reject this last phase of neo-individualism. Rather, I think with Vico that it is inconceivable that we could ever constitute society in the will to contract all human relations outside of the great historical body of our family and civic society. Here, then, I appeal to *a familied history without which there cannot be any one of us*. The telling of that history goes beyond the confessional practices of today's advice columns as much as it does our official historical writing. It cannot be divided into the history of great men, nor can it be assigned to the new histories of women and children. Each of us keeps this familied history and in all things we are a witness to it. For it is holy:

> A history of any one must be a long one, slowly it comes out of them from their beginning to their ending, slowly you can see it in them the nature and the mixtures in them, slowly everything comes out from each one in the kind of repeating each one does in the different parts and kinds of living they have in them, slowly then the history of them comes out from them, slowly then any one who looks well at any one will have the history of the whole of that one. Slowly the history of each one comes out of each one. Sometime then there will be a history of every one. (Stein, 1934: 128)

Today we witness a growing movement in post-industrial societies to redefine bodily experience as nothing more than sheer labor power, to be managed as the docile instrument of commercial, educational, and medical practice. To come to terms with such a movement, we must critically rethink the analytic practices of economics, politics, medicine, and the social sciences, a process we shall attempt in the following chapters. Social scientists tend to study disembodied persons, preferring to work with quantitative data or interview schedules. It is the function of much sociological discourse to enact a ritual of decontamination between the scientist and his subject. It is essential that professional sociologists resist the look in the eyes of the sick, the poor, and the aimless who turn their questions back upon them (O'Neill, 1972). It is essential that we social scientists remind ourselves of the fundamentally communicative body that is the moral basis of all society and of the practice of any social science. We cannot escape life among others. Our bodies commit us from the first moment of life to the company of those who have grown up and who, in turn, oblige themselves to care for our physical well-being. Of course, the aim of the care we receive as children is to bring us to care for ourselves, to free us from the dependency of an immature body and an uneducated mind. Thus, the satisfaction of our bodily needs is never intended by those who care for us to yield in us a merely selfish pleasure. Human care initiates us into a *tradition of caring* whereby we learn to give back what we ourselves have received. This is an essential condition of civic society. Unless it is realized, we are threatened with the prospect of a society – which I examine later – where there is little genuine sociability but mostly the exchange of selfish and calculated interests between individuals who sense no deeper bond among them. Rather, sociability rests upon our reciprocal experience and upon the vulnerability and openness to one another that arises from the kind of communicative life we enjoy as embodied beings.

Our bodies, then, are the fine instruments of both the smaller and the larger society in which we live. Human dexterity is such that we are capable of an infinitely wide use of tools which in turn feed in and out of the huge divisions of labor that are the basis of society in its broadest sense. Our bodies are also the warm instrument of the most intimate associations we know. In particular, we make special use of our bodies to celebrate our sheer sociability whenever we dress, adorn our necks, arms, wrists, and eyes, paint our cheeks and lips, or exchange smiles, kisses, and handshakes. Thus, whenever our bodies are unwell, we generally beg off parties and social gatherings, just as our general commitment to sociability requires otherwise weight-conscious people to eat and drink on behalf of others, with mild protests, more than is good for themselves. If the body is the instrument of our commitment to various types of social engagements and tasks, it is also the instrument of our refusal of society on particular occasions and in specific ways. Small children will scream and kick, refuse to eat or sleep, make a mess, and get themselves dirty to express their dislike for parental wishes. Prisoners and psychiatric patients, not to mention adolescents, will do the same. Here the body is the instrument of refusal and rejection, just as from the standpoint of authority its compliance is the instrument of order. Hence the ultimate social sanction is incarceration, confining the body, and submitting it to pain, torture, hunger, and perhaps even execution (Scarry, 1985). Revolutionaries, rebels, heretics, delinquents, criminals, and even the sick all risk their bodies in some way as the price of contesting society's official bodies and their established practices.

We are continuously caught up and engaged in *the embodied look of things*, especially in the look of others and of ourselves. Although philosophers and moralists have decried our attachment to appearances and superficialities, as sociologists we cannot ignore the elaborate social construction of embodied appearances in which we are necessarily engaged as persons. Indeed, it is here that we touch upon two very basic aspects of our social life. It is through our senses that we first appreciate and evaluate others, immediately shaping our own positive, pleasurable, and trusting responses, or else our negative, fearful, and avoiding reactions. What we see, hear, and feel of other persons is the first basis for our interaction with them. This is the carnal ground of our social knowledge. Because *society is never a disembodied spectacle*, we engage in social interaction from the very start on the basis of sensory and aesthetic impressions:

> Saying that I have a body is thus a way of saying that I can be seen as an object and that I try to be seen as a subject, that another can be my master or my slave, so that shame and shamelessness express the dialectic of the plurality of consciousness, and have a metaphysical significance. (Merleau-Ponty, 1962: 167)

The look of the other person is the *prima facie* ground of our knowledge of him or her. We do not engage from the start in endless doubts about whether appearances are deceiving. As embodied persons, whose needs are not easily suspended, we are obliged for all practical purposes to treat appearances as realities.

We seek out other bodies in society as mirrors of ourselves – the second basic feature of social life. And this is because our own bodies are the permeable ground of all social behavior; our bodies are the very flesh of society. Charles Horton Cooley (1964) spoke of this permeable ground in nearly bodily terms when he drew the attention of sociologists and psychologists to the notion of the *looking glass self*. What we see in the mirror is what others see. Here is *the incarnate bond between self and society*. What sociologists call the socialization process, namely the bringing up of an infant or child by those who care for it in accordance with the prevailing standards of behavior, rests upon the infant's *visceral knowledge* of what is required of it, conveyed as early as its feeding, cuddling, handling, toileting experiences with its mother. From its earliest moments, and long before it can apprentice to the rules of perception, language, and conduct, the child's body resonates with its social experience. The warm community of the child's world 'somehow' – being precise would require a psychoanalysis – stands as our first world, the measure of all our other worldly engagements. What Cooley called the 'looking glass self' is actually part of the complex acquisition of what is now called the *body image*, which involves passing through a crucial *mirror stage* that enables the infant to become aware of the distinction between its experience of its *own body* and the other person's experience of it as *a body* (O'Neill, 1989). Thus from infancy we acquire the ability to mirror our intentions in the facial and linguistic expressions of our mother as the basis for their further elaboration according to mother's and later others' sense of their meaning.

Since human embodiment functions to create the most fundamental bond between the self and society, we might now briefly look at some of its consequences in settings of adult life that may at first sight seem strange or trivial and yet be of enormous consequence in the lives of those committed to the embodied universe of social appearances. No society seems content to leave the biophysical body outside the symbolic system whereby members communicate to one another their age, gender, marital status, sexual availability, social standing, and the like (Bourdieu, 1977). It is in this light that we can understand that the elaborate cosmetic and grooming practices in which persons of all sorts are involved for a considerable amount of the day, at enormous cost and by means of the strangest of rituals, are a necessary expression of their commitment to prevailing social mores and values. We must think of the detail of such practices as body painting, scarification, adornment, hair-cutting and dressing, washing, perfuming, deodorizing, covering and concealing various bodily parts, as a resource for the incessant *eye-work* (O'Neill, 1975) whereby we make the way people appear constituent features of social reality. Thus, a good deal of the information we need in order to be properly oriented in the social settings in which we find ourselves is visually available in the form of *body advertisements* practiced by the most ordinary persons, and only accentuated by models. It is important, then, to connect the otherwise bewildering variety of these techniques of the body to the two basic functions of embodiment and the social self we have previously discussed. Moreover, it cannot be sufficiently stressed how these bodily readings represent massive, vulgarly available competences whose work achieves an *incarnate society*, that is, the embodied reality of everyday life.

Of course, our carnal knowledge of embodied persons is always defeasible in the light of our further experience with them. And, as we find ourselves in situations further and further away from intimate, friendly and familial relations – not that these cannot be hard to disentangle – we need to acquire a larger sense of institutional and role requirements in order to make sense of the behavior around us and what it requires on our part. In particular, we are now much more aware of the *sexual contract* (Pateman, 1988; 1989) which codes families within patriarchal society (Turner, 1984) and restricts women's citizenship. Thus there has been a considerable revision of political economy of gender, of intra-family, marital and parental relationships that has considerably expanded our earlier grasp of body politics.

1

The World's Body

Today we are busy giving a shape to a world that is no longer our own. Such, at any rate, is the complaint of many artists and social scientists who speak of our world alienation or, as I see it, a process of *negative anthropomorphism*. We are no longer reflected in our work, our institutions, or our environment. The abstraction of modern experience is based upon the removal of the human shape in favor of the measured – number, line, sign, code, index. Everywhere anthropomorphism, the creative force in the civic shaping of human beings, is in retreat. Such a fate would be unthinkable were it not in fact intelligible as a strategy whereby humankind has redesigned its own body, its family, the body politic, the economy and nature in order to exercise a form of domination over the world and itself that threatens to be the last of all metamorphoses. At the same time there are indications that, despite our unprecedented power over the universe and ourselves, we still feel the need for the bond of affection, the ties of local community and for the familiar resonance of our own kind in smaller worlds of ordinary things fitted more cosily even if more shabbily to the human frame (O'Neill, 1974).

The decline of anthropomorphism represents a huge shift in our cosmography. Whereas formerly people could think the universe through their bodies and their own bodies through the universe – each to each a cosmic model of totality and proportion – today they must think systems and structures without embodied subjects (Barkan, 1975; Conger, 1922). Just as robots do the work in science-fiction systems, so literary systems do the work of artists confined now to clever ventriloquism no better than that of the official language which subordinates social life to bureaucratic systems. In all modern systems we abstract from embodiment, time, and community (Lévi-Strauss, 1966). The promise is that these embodied limits of the human polity will be transcended, or else marginalized, in the release of collective energy and control exercised through imaginative science fictions whose power lies in their ability to deal with evolutionary levels of complexity and openness beyond the scope of anthropomorphic thought.

I do not mean to reject nonanthropocentric science. Rather, my purpose is to keep alive the ground from which science starts and to which its promise is beholden. I shall argue, therefore, that *the ground of universal science is the world's body*. It might be claimed that anthropomorphism is only *faute de mieux* the source of primitive peoples' cosmology. I would rather argue with Vico that the rationalist reconstruction of the cosmos is possible only on the ground of that first *poetic logic* whereby people thought the world with their bodies:

> The human mind is naturally inclined by the senses to see itself externally in the body and only with great difficulty does it come to understand itself by means of reflection. This axiom gives us the universal principle of etymology in all languages: words are carried over from bodies and from the properties of bodies to signify the institutions of the mind and spirit. (Vico, 1970: paras 236–7)

The magnificent insight in Vico's *The New Science* is that human society could not have been created from the start according to rationalist principles. Rather, Vico, like Durkheim much later, saw that our ancestors necessarily thought the world with their gendered bodies, or with their families, since these and not the mind are the ground of all rational categories. Modern science can hardly overestimate the importance of the legacy of archaic cosmological thought. It is impossible to imagine an unmapped universe waiting for the rationalist sciences to domesticate it. Our ancestors would more likely have died from fear had they not from the very beginning anthropomorphized and thereby domesticated everything around them. The distance between the categorical schemas of modern science and those of our early ancestors is tiny compared with the inconceivable gap between a world anthropomorphized and sheer chaos. In short, it is the very continuity between modern and primitive thought that was guaranteed when our ancestors thought the world in terms of their gendered bodies and families:

> The first logical categories were social categories; the first classes were classes of men, into which things were integrated. It was because men were grouped, and thought of themselves in the form of groups, that in their ideas they grasped other things, and in the beginning the two modes of groupings were merged to the point of being indistinct. Moieties were the first genera; clans the first species. Things were thought to be integral parts of society and it was their place in society which determined their place in nature. (Durkheim and Mauss, 1963: 82–3)

Thus human beings think nature and society with their bodies. That is to say they first think the world and society as one giant body. In turn, the divisions of the body yield the divisions of the world and of society of humans and of animals. Primitive classification followed an *embodied logic* of division of gender and kinship and replication, which, far from being unscientific or irrational, was the very foundation on which later, abstract and rationalized modes of categorization could be developed in both the human and the natural sciences. It can be argued, therefore, that the rational class concepts are not simply a unilinear development from the first imaginative universals but that both are structural elements of an inseparable historical and social matrix. The myths of the first people are not the poor science of modern men: nor are they mere allegories or poetic embellishments of truths otherwise achieved by science. They are the indispensable origins of human order and commonwealth apart from which the later achievements of humanism and scientism are impossible conceits. In other words, anthropomorphism – and not rationalism – is the necessary first stage of the human world.

> It is noteworthy that in all languages the greater part of the expressions relating to inanimate things are formed by metaphor from the human body and its parts and from the human senses and passions. Thus, head for top or beginning; the brow and shoulders of a hill; the eyes of needles and of potatoes; mouth for any opening; the lip of a cup or pitcher; the teeth of a rake, a saw, a comb; the beard of wheat; the tongue of a shoe; the gorge of a river; a neck of land; an arm of the sea; the hands of a clock; heart for center (the Latins used *umbilicus*, navel, in this sense); the belly of a sail; foot for end or bottom; the flesh of fruits; a vein of rock or mineral; the blood of grapes for wine; the bowels of the earth. Heaven or the sea smiles; the wind whistles; the waves murmur; a body groans under a great weight. The farmers of Latium used to say the fields were thirsty, bore fruit, were swollen with grain; and our rustics speak of plants making love, vines going mad, resinous trees weeping. Innumerable other examples could be collected from all languages. All of which is a consequence of our axiom (120) that man in his ignorance makes himself the rule of the universe, for in the examples cited he has made of himself an entire world. So that, as rational metaphysics teaches that man becomes all things by understanding them (*homo intelligendo fit omnia*), this imaginative metaphysics shows that man becomes all things by *not* understanding them (*homo non intelligendo fit omnia*); and perhaps the latter proposition is truer than the former, for when man understands he extends his mind and takes in the things, but when he does not understand he makes the things out of himself and becomes them by transforming himself into them. (Vico, 1970, para 405)

What Vico conjectured may be seen in the story-shaped world of the Dogon, a West African people who were among the last to come under French colonial rule. Their distance from us should recede as we listen through them to our own need for a storyable world. Indeed, we never go without such stories. Even in today's space fictions what is extra-territorial is really our need of a home and a place for our selves and not only for the extra-terrestrial creature E.T., as our children recognize.

To the Dogon the world is a great body. It is moreover, a communicative body and the 'word' is the key to everything in the world's body. The Dogon view of the world is anthropomorphic; at every level it reflects the imagery of the gendered body – its minerals and plants, as well as its artifacts, are parts of a gigantic body (Calame-Griaule, 1965; Turner, 1974). The world's body and the world's speech are inseparable. Its story is told to us by Ogotemmêli (Griaule, 1965), once a hunter, now an old and blind villager of Lower Ogol. Just as the God Amma threw the stars out into space, so he threw from his hand a lump of clay that fell and flattened out in the shape of a woman's body. The anthill is the sexual organ of the world's body and its clitoris is a termite hill. Being lonely Amma desired the world's body. The termite hill resisted Amma's approaches, and so Amma cut it down. From this disorderly union the jackal was born, a symbol of Amma's difficulties. Thereafter, Amma had further intercourse with his earthwife. Water, the divine seed, entered the earth's womb and so the androgynous twins, Nummo, were born and went to heaven to receive instruction from their father. From there, they saw their mother-earth, naked and speechless. They therefore came down from heaven with the fibers of plants to clothe the earth in a skirt. This was done not only to save her modesty but to restore order through speech. The fibers of the earth's dress were channels of moisture full of Nummo, which is the warm air upon which speech floats. Just as the human body is made up of the elements of water, earth, air and fire, so too is the body of speech. Saliva is water without which speech is dry; air supports the sound of speech; earth gives it its weight and significance, and fire gives speech its warmth. Thus the body's insides are projected outside in the body of speech, each proportioned to the other, like a garment. The Dogon say that *to be naked is to be speechless*.

The Nummo, however, could see that the descent of the eight original androgynous twins was not secure. They therefore came down again to dwell in the earth's womb. The male Nummo took the place of the termite-hill clitoris and the female Nummo's womb became part of the earth's womb. In time, the eldest of the ancestor pairs came to the anthill womb occupied by Nummo and sank into it feet first, leaving behind him his food bowl, a symbol of his human body. Inside the earth's womb, he became water and word and then was expelled up into heaven. All eight ancestors went through this metamorphosis. But the seventh ancestor, the symbol of the perfect union of the male element, which is three, and the female element, which is four, was given the mastery of language. This time the language was clearer than the first word that had clothed the earth and was meant for everyone, not just a few initiates. The word of the seventh ancestor contained the progress of the world. He therefore began to occupy the whole of the earth's womb for his purposes. His lips widened to the edge of the anthill which in turn widened so that the earth's womb became a mouth, and pointed teeth appeared to the number of eighty or ten (the number of the fingers) for each ancestor. At sunrise on the appointed day the seventh ancestor spirit spat out eighty threads of cotton, his upper and lower teeth holding the warp and woof and his whole face working to weave the tissue (text) of the second Word:

> The words that the Spirit uttered filled all the interstices of the stuff: they were woven in the threads, and formed part and parcel of the cloth. They were the cloth, and the cloth was the Word. That is why the woven material is called *soy*, which means 'It is the spoken word.' *Soy* also means 'seven,' as the Spirit who spoke as he wove was seventh in the series of ancestors. (Griaule, 1965: 28)

It was, however, through the ant that the seventh ancestor passed on the Word, and she in turn relayed it to the men born after the earth had lost her clitoris. Prior to this time, people had lived in simple holes in the earth, like the lairs of animals. They now began to build in the shape of anthills, making rooms with connecting passages, and they began to store food and to mold great teeth of clay around the entrances to their dwellings, like the teeth of the earth's womb:

> The ant at the same time revealed the words it had heard and the man repeated them. Thus there was recreated by human lips the concept of life in motion, of

the transposition of forces, of the efficacy of the breath of the Spirit, which the seventh ancestor had created; and thus the interlacing of warp and weft enclosed the same words, the new instructions which became the heritage of mankind and was handed on from generation to generation of weavers to the accompaniment of the clapping of the shuttle and the creaking of the block, which they call the 'creaking of the word'. (ibid.: 29)

Due to a further breach of order in Heaven, the Dogon received the third Word, which is built into the Granary of Pure Earth, the model for all the village granaries. The construction of each granary reflects the elements and stages in the construction of the world. Moreover, its arrangement perfects that of the anthill, which had been the model for humans' first dwellings above ground. The Granary of Pure Earth was built after the shape of a woven basket, with a circular top and square base in which was carried the earth and clay from which the Word was built. This shape was inverted, however, giving the Granary of Pure Earth a circular bottom representing the Sun, and a square top representing the Sky with a circular opening to represent the Moon. Each of the four sides was cut into by ten steps, the tread of each being female and the riser male. Each of the four sides represented a constellation of animals and stars. The north stairway was for men and fishes; the south stairway was for domestic animals, the east for birds, and the west for wild animals, vegetables, and insects. The granary was entered from the sixth step on the north side, just wide enough to let a man's body pass. This opening was called the mouth of the granary and the rest of the granary was called the world's belly. The interior was divided into four partitioned chambers above and below numbering eight in all. The eight compartments contained the eight seeds given to the eight ancestors: little millet, white millet, dark millet, female millet, beans, sorrel, rice, and Digitaria. The eight compartments also represented the eight organs of the Spirit of water comparable to human organs, with the addition of the gizzard because the Spirit moves as fast as a bird. The organs were displayed in the following order: stomach, gizzard, heart, small liver, spleen, intestines, great liver, gall bladder. In the center of the granary there stood a round jar, symbolizing the womb; inside, a second smaller jar, containing oil, represented the fetus. On top of the second jar stood an even smaller jar containing perfume, and on this stood two cups:

> All the eight organs were held in place by the outer walls and the inner partitions which symbolized the skeleton. The four uprights ending in the corners of the square roof were the arms and legs. Thus the granary was like a woman, lying on her back (representing the sun) with her arms and legs raised and supporting the roof (representing the sky). The two legs were on the north side, and the door at the sixth step marked the sexual parts. (ibid.: 39)

Not only was the Granary of Pure Earth a model of the world's body; it also functioned in its parts to reflect the processes of reproduction, sexually and materially whereby the world's body renews itself and the Dogon people:

> The granary and all it contained was therefore a picture of the world-system of the new order, and the way in which this system worked was represented by the functioning of the internal organs. These organs absorbed symbolic

nourishment which passed along the usual channels of the digestion and the circulation of blood. From compartments 1 and 2 (stomach and gizzard) the symbolical food passed into compartment 6 (the intestines) and from there into all the others in the form of blood and lastly breath, ending in the liver and the gall bladder. The breath is a vapour, a form of water, which maintains and is indeed the principle of life. (Calame-Griaule, 1965: 39)

The Word of the Dogon, like the seed of the earth's body, is carried in their clavicles, which are called the granary of the little millet, the food that saved the people in times of famine. The clavicles are the guardians of the Dogon's life force, personality and speech. It is in the water of the clavicles that the symbolic grains germinate, generating the individual's energy according to his or her rank, role, and activity in the community. The production of speech involves the body working like a smithy: the lungs pumping in and out the air, the heart warming the water. The spleen is the hammer hitting against the stomach; the liver is the anvil; the curved intestine breaks up the food and the words, giving the best to the joints in order to strengthen the body. The uvula represents the smithy's pincers 'grasping' the words on the way into the mouth and guiding them out. Having forged the warm moist sounds of speech inside his body like a blacksmith, the speaker still has to turn these sounds into intelligible speech. The work of giving the sounds their specific and relative character is compared to the work of weaving. The mouth is like a loom weaving intelligible speech suited to all the various occasions, functions, roles, and activities of Dogon life. The nerves of the cranium and the jaws are compared to the rear and front posts that support the loom/mouth, the teeth are the comb, and the tongue the shuttle going back and forth. The throat, actually the vocal chords, is like the pulley that makes the characteristic creak of the loom. The rise and fall of the uvula are compared to the warp and the words themselves to the weaver's threads. The act of speaking – talking, listening, talking – resembles the back-and-forth movements of the hands with the shuttle of the feet moving up and down to alter the height of the threads. The crisscrossing of speech and weaving is also reflected in the continual shift from high to low tones, from female to male sounds, which spell out the endless dialogue of the sexes in the alternating music and dances of the Dogon – just as in the crack of the looms that weave together the Dogon costumes, customs, and community.

Our ancestors, then, were incredibly inventive in portraying a world in which they had a recognizable place. This, in my opinion, is the same creative impulse that we admire in classical civilization and its legacy to Europe. The continuity of anthropomorphic thought in the West from the pre-Socratics to the Renaissance and in Eastern as well as African and Amerindian societies justifies us in preserving a universal mode of thought essential to our humanity. In other words, I think that anthropomorphism is a potentially radical heritage preserved in our mythology and poetry reminding us of fundamental ties between the shape of humankind and the shape of society and the universe, each mirrored in the other. As pictured in Plato's *Timaeus*, literate society still thinks itself as a world body containing all other bodies, thereby bringing each of the four families – the heavenly gods (which include the stars, planets, earth), the birds of the air, the fishes of the sea, and the animals on land – closer to one another and to the intelligible Form of the divine Creator. In accordance with this Form, the Demiurge fashions the world's material body, a perfect combination of the four elements held in friendly proportion:

> Now the frame of the world took up the whole of each of these four; he who put it together made it consist of all the fire and water and air and earth, leaving no part or power of any one of them outside. This was his intent: first, that it might be in the fullest measure a living being whole and complete, of complete parts; next, that it might be single, nothing left over, out of which such another might come into being; and moreover that it might be free from age and sickness. For he perceived that, if a body be composite, when hot things and cold and all things that have strong powers beset that body and attack it from without, they bring it to untimely dissolution and cause it to waste away by bringing upon it sickness and age. For this reason and so considering, he fashioned it as a single whole consisting of all these wholes, complete and free from age and sickness. (Plato, *Timaeus*, 1959, 32c–33b)

We should not read Plato's *Timaeus* without sensing its similarity with the myths of Ogotemmêli. The sublimity of their common conception of the world's body makes them comparable. The Demiurge orders chaos with his body which in turn reflects the order and disorder sown in the universe. The Forms of Truth, Beauty and Justice are thereby a grounded cosmography precisely because they are written into the body which is 'framed like a heaven to include them'. Thus the human body is the bridge for all microcosmic and macrocosmic exchanges, as in the Babylonian systems of astrobiology and astrogeography which thrive in our own newspaper and magazine horoscopes. These systems of thought are not to be regarded as the country cousins of psychology and predictive testing. They are, rather, *holy systems*. That is to say they are concerned with the parallels of wholeness between the planets, the stars, and the human body. The zodiacal and planetary systems pair anatomy and cosmography to give us forecast or free play according to our fantasy:

> The planetary system is joined with the human body not astronomically but by the metamorphosis of the planets into gods who have human form and personality. If we carry this system beyond its originally narrow imaginative limits, the Cosmos can form an external stage on which dramas can be acted out and then mirrored in the working of our anatomy. If we restrict ourselves purely to the plane of anatomy, these dramas are as predictable as all planetary motion; but with the attribution of anthropomorphic significance to the planets via the lives of the gods, the dramas within one human anatomy or among various people have a greater potential field of variety. (Barkan, 1975: 24)

A nice depiction of our astral body and its dramas is to be found in Geoffroy Tory's image of *encyclopedic man* (Figure 1.1), whose proportions are identified with the nine muses and the seven liberal arts, and who has the Virtues in his hand and feet. In this image, heaven and earth are harmonized in the humane arts, which in turn repeat a harmony between mind and body, as well as between the individual and society, albeit at the expense of any such figuration of woman's body, though not interior of her spiritual body.

In natural philosophy, theology, mysticism, law and poetry, we constantly find recourse to the body metaphor as a key to the principles of order and hierarchy in society and the universe, and we shall examine something of this in the imagery of the body politic (Chapter 3). The literal and figurative traditions of microcosmography are characteristic of medieval and Renaissance thought:

> In the literary image of the body as microcosm, the literal and figurative visions are joined; but in the history of natural philosophy through the Middle Ages and the Renaissance, the figurative tradition remained independent from the literal and very much more in the mainstream of thought. The figurative view of man as microcosm arises out of a great variety of philosophical traditions and periods, but it is always composed of two parts: a *method*, the metaphoric imagination that transforms a non-human phenomenon into an equivalent within human experience, and a *content*, the idea that man contains everything which he can perceive in the world around him. These are the presuppositions of humanism, whether classical, medieval, or Renaissance. The method praises man's mind, and the content praises his condition. (Barkan, 1975: 28)

In the Renaissance, Pico della Mirandola attributed humanity's glory to our body believing that it is only our physiognomy which is freely determinable in respect of heaven and earth. Only human beings can become an angel or a beast; or, as we might now add, a cyborg. Every one of these options, however, arises for us only inasmuch as we are uniquely embodied beings. Thereafter, the mind may figuratively contain the whole universe, *homo omnis creatura*. Such is the imagery that fed the religion, science, law and poetry of the world until Copernicus, Galileo, and Newton displaced anthropomorphic cosmography with modern physics. Then the world's body became remote, a thing indifferent to the human body and to human fables of cosmic influence. Bacon and Locke reduced the body to its five senses – the unhistorical open receptors of Newton's natural world. Under these auspices the human eye and mind are merely mirrors of the empirical world. They are to see and dream no further. Nor is there any need. God's clockwork runs without him and ours should do the same with proper education, for our bodies and senses operate like any other natural phenomenon.

It is Blake, of course, who challenges the Lockean philosophy of the five senses in order to restore once again that imaginative body which is the ground upon which we may resist equally naturalism and supernaturalism (Frosch, 1974). Blake struggles against the divisions and natural anatomy of the vegetative body, against its shrinkage and decay, against its fallen senses, sacrificed to sin, chastity and abhorrence, unsatisfied and self-destructive. The philosopher's body is a fallen body natural and perspectival, fragmented, yearning for wholeness through the radically passive domination of

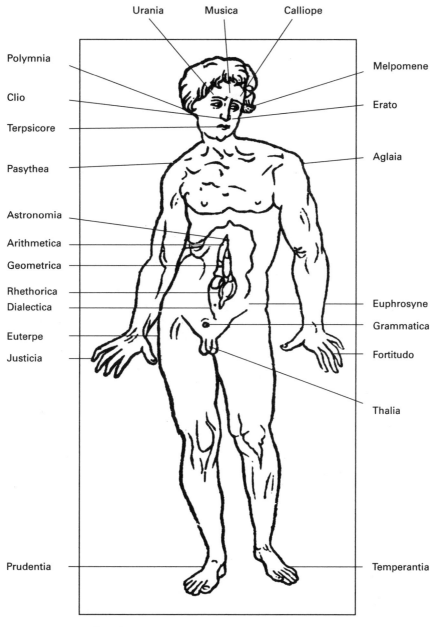

LHOMME SCIENTIFIQVE

Figure 1.1   *Encyclopedic Man*

the world and ourselves to which we are mostly mere witnesses. The *eye-culture* cripples self-consciousness, observing it like a thing, *pars extra partes*, externalized, cast out. The natural body binds itself to the real and the present, above all to sexuality and property contracting itself to a point, turned away from the universe within the fourfold imaginative body of Albion:

> And every Man stood Fourfold. Each Four Faces had. One to the West
> One toward the East. One to the South One to the North. the Horses Fourfold
> And the dim Chaos brightened beneath, above, around! Eyed as the Peacock
> According to the Human Nerves of Sensation, the Four Rivers of the Water of Life
> South Stood the Nerves of the Eye. East in Rivers of bliss the Nerves of the
> Expansive Nostrils West, flowd the Parent Sense the Tongue. North stood
> The labyrinthine Ear. Circumscribing & Circumcising the excrementitious
> Musk & Covering into Vacuum evaporating revealing the lineaments of Man
> Driving outward the Body of Death in an Eternal Death & Resurrection
> Awaking it to Life among the Flowers of Beulah reJoicing in Unity
> In the Four Senses in the Outline the Circumference & Form, for ever
> In Forgiveness of Sins which is Self Annihilation. It is the Covenant of Jehovah.
>
> (Blake, 1982: 257, *Jerusalem*, 98, 12–23)

It is important not to reduce the autosymbolic work of the body to what Mircea Eliade (1978) calls 'the world sexualized'. The anthropomorphization of the world is fashioned from all parts of the body. That is why I invoke the *gendered or familied body*, to be clear that I refer to a kinship of men, women and children, of past and future generations joined through a rich treasury of affiliation, place, and common sense. This is the first body of society – the *wild body* of all human culture (O'Neill, 1975). The gendered body is not the sexualized body. Otto Rank has argued – despite Freud – that the anthropomorphic projection of the body represents a concern with wholeness and identity rather than with re-generation, which is a transition-phase in creation:

> Those theories which have made out that artistic creativity is the expression of the sexual impulse have only made use of a transition phase of man as creature to secularize the conception of man as creator. Indeed, this latter conception itself, as manifested in the idea of God, amounts to nothing less than an objec-tification of a creative urge that is no longer satisfied with self-reproduction, but must proceed to create an entire cosmos as the setting of that self. (Rank, 1968: 134–5)

Thus the liver, the navel, the head, the mouth, the upper vertebrae, the entrails, and the womb have all been symbolic sources in the search for microcosms of the universe. By a circuitous route from animal worship, from Babylon through Egypt and Greece into Christianity there occurred a double shift – microcosmically from the 'lower-body' culture to the 'upper-head' culture and, macrocosmically from terrestrial to celestial cultures. According to this pattern, the world breathes as a body breathes, each inhabited, as it were, by a material and a spiritual soul, or breath of life. The Greek *psyche* and the Latin *anima* both mean the breath-soul, the visible, tangible life that comes and goes, moving from the lower to the higher body until the intellect and reason become the seat of the soul. By the same token, the world becomes flesh, logos of the world, which is God.

Lévi-Strauss (1966) has pointed out that we cannot separate ourselves from so-called primitives (our archaic ancestors) on the ground that they lack the interest that we have in the objective classification of things, events, and relationships from which science is built. The cognitive competence exhibited by the first human beings with respect to the categories of animals, vegetables, fruits, and minerals in their environment is proverbial. It is, moreover, an active, pragmatic competence and not merely a passive knowledge, confined to esoteric dictionaries. By the same token, these categorial systems exhibit an intrinsic preference for order over chaos; in this regard primitive thought is in a continuous line with science. Nor should we be deceived by the practice of the first humans of according the attributes of holiness, contamination, and taboo where science might speak only of 'goodness of fit', or adequate generalization. There is little difference here. Things are holy inasmuch as they find their place, observe the norms of their kind, and do not contravene or threaten the orderliness in which people have an interest if their affairs are to prosper. We must rather look upon archaic classifications as anticipations of modern science whose own strategy was to abstract from the sensory world in which early humans first found themselves and where, as Vico tells us, they were obliged to think with their sensory minds. The achievements of the first men and women in bringing forth pottery, weaving, metals, agriculture, the domestication of animals, as well as the rites of birth, marriage, and burial are enormous. It is impossible to conceive these elements of civilization as the result of anything else than a human preference for order and calculability concelebrated in the least resource involved in its production. Here I refer to the art, myth, and religion that recollect the creation of order. We therefore cannot ignore that neolithic people accumulated a long scientific tradition which still lies at the basis of modern natural science. Indeed, Lévi-Strauss argues that what is involved here are two complementary traditions of scientific inquiry differentiated according to the degree to which they are closer to or remote from 'sensible intuition', or what with Vico I have called *sensory mind*:

> Myths and rites are far from being, as has often been held, the product of man's 'myth-making faculty,' turning its back upon reality. Their principal value is indeed to preserve until the present time the remains of methods of observation and reflection which were (and no doubt still are) precisely adapted to discoveries of a certain type: those which nature authorized from the starting point of a speculative organization and exploitation of the sensible world in sensible terms. This science of the concrete was necessarily restricted by its essence to results other than those destined to be achieved by the exact natural sciences but it was no less scientific and its results no less genuine. They were secured ten thousand years earlier and still remain at the basis of our own civilization. (Lévi-Strauss, 1966: 16)

So far from being an early stage of thought, or one that might be allowed to atrophy with modern advances, those arts of sensible intuition Lévi-Strauss refers to under the notion of *bricolage* are what make scientific practice possible. The bricoleur is not tied to the distinctive materials or procedures of a given craft. Rather, s/he moves into a neighboring craft whenever the need to improvise arises, a need that he is able to see within the materials at hand although they are not explicitly designed for incorporation in his constructions. The bricoleur is an independent agent with respect to the conceptual and instrumental sets s/he has at hand, being capable of turning their built-in constraints to new combinations that surpass the limits of the old while respecting them. Mythical thinking and scientific thought both involve intellectual bricolage. And this common root is more significant than the outworn notion of the evolutionary distance between science and myth construction. Given any ready-made materials, the bricoleur may be said to create structures from events, or necessity from contingency, whereas the scientist creates events through the structures s/he imposes upon nature. In either case, artifacts intervene, whether as models or miniaturizations, in which the part/whole structures of the object are experimented with in a synthesis of natural and social events. And in terms of another analogy science is like a game inasmuch as both create events through the imposition of a structure, whereas bricolage and myth resemble each other in treating historical and social events as indestructible pieces for recombined structures of the new and the same.

In this and the following chapters, then, I am urging us to think of the future shape of the world, nature, society and the human family by recollecting our past creativity in self-shaping. To make the future livable, we must not listen to those who seek to sever it from the past and to put the future, so to speak, in automatic gear. Our future is not something we can allow to be thrust upon us like some 'new' detergent. The elitist visionaries of future technology reduce the human future to an element in our general culture of passive consumerism, to a promise of passive health and happiness. The ordinary person, who is each of us most of the time, needs to see that modern society and its future technologies of the mind, body and political economy have not really come a long way without the enormous legacy of past human efforts. As ordinary people, therefore, we must insist upon the recollection of our cultural history through which we have brought ourselves to the frontier of modernism. We must insist upon our kinship with the world, with nature and wild life, and with the varied family cultures of the earth, realizing that there is far less distance between our past and the present than between today and a tomorrow without us. It is this creed that I consider to be the deep structure of anthropomorphism. As such it is neither naive nor nostalgic. Of course, some might reach the opposite conclusion by seizing on the weakness and fallibility of human projection. From this standpoint, anthropomorphism is the last error of a nerveless humanism unable to live in a cosmos that refuses to mirror us. Here the paradox is that the currently fashionable antihumanism of social and literary systems without agents runs counter to the participatory epistemology of contemporary physics, which has abandoned the clockwork world of its early modern paradigm (O'Neill, 1995). Modern physics has restored the fundamental effects of embodied perception in its theory of knowledge. The complicity between the *embodied knower* and the objects of scientific knowledge requires that anthropomorphism be regarded as a constitutive feature of modern knowledge rather than as an idol of human ignorance.

Among those who have realized the implications of modern quantum physics, there is an urgent appeal for the renewal of holistic thinking (Berman, 1981). Of course, this means flying in the face of all the liberal-warnings about the errors and monstrosities of totalitarianism. But the real issue is one of whether we respect and conserve the world's body. Here the real enemy is neo-individualism as we have marketed it in North America and Western Europe (I do not mean to imply that the industrialized socialist economies have been any the less dangerous to the human future of mankind). It is as easy as it is dangerous to beguile ourselves with the endless novelties of a future that will be produced without us. Everywhere we turn, there are proposals to redesign life, the mind, emotions, behavior, our work and living places in order to suit us to a high-tech future that will increasingly dispose of us, adding us to the world's already marginalized peoples whose diseased, famined, and homeless bodies never find peace and dignity on terms with the machine societies by whom they are dominated and discarded.

We have surveyed an elaborate cosmography constructed upon the articulations and vital functions of our communicative body. This conception of the world's body may seem remote to a society built upon the industrial conquest of nature. Yet whenever the excesses of this domination of nature are observed, as they are today, it becomes natural once again to remind ourselves of our kinship with the world's body – and thereby of our need to respect what is left of its wholeness. Radical anthropomorphism requires that we think the future shape of human beings according to a rule of civic conservation that places nature before life, yet life before society and the family before ourselves. To practice this civic rule, we must think the future as the present in order not to disconnect it from our everyday living and the fundamental ground of moral criticism which is rooted in our carnal knowledge of the good and evil we practice upon one another. It is in this sense, then, that the following chapters provide a backward look upon our future orientation. We are not, however, proposing an archetypal history of the civilizing process (Elias, 1978). Rather, we are following Vico's concept of cultural matrix whose obviation (Wagner, 1986) results in its reconfiguration of the core symbols of religion, society and politics to rethink our altered circumstance and kinship (Strathern, 1992).

2

Social Bodies

When we turn from the world's body to look at the smaller world of society and kinship, we are struck to find that people have also conceived the relation between their individual lives and the institutions of society in terms of the imagery of the human body. Lévi-Strauss observes:

> The Australian tribes of the Drysdale River, in Northern Kimberley divide all kinship relations, which together compose the social 'body', into five categories named after a part of the body or a muscle. Since a stranger must not be questioned, he announces his kinship by moving the relevant muscle. In this case, too, therefore, the total system of social relations, itself bound up with a system of the universe, can be projected on to the anatomical plane. (Lévi-Strauss, 1966: 168–9)

It is a conceit of ours that if society rules us at all it does so in our minds rather than in our bodies. We are, of course, enormously ambivalent about either side of these controls. We prefer to think that we rule our bodies rather than being ruled by them – without giving much thought to the body politic implicit in this conception of order (which we shall consider in the following chapter). Likewise, we are aware of society's rule over us. But we prefer to think that society operates upon us intellectually and consensually rather than directly upon our bodies, which suggests a more slavish relation (MacRae, 1975). In the final chapter we shall look at some specific issues in the exercise of modern *biopower*, or the biotechnological redefinition of mind-body behavior basic to the modern state. For the moment, however, I want to focus on the argument that social order in general is never just a cognitive construct or an abstract system of rules and categories to which individuals conform, whether freely or unfreely. I shall argue, instead, that there is an *embodied logic* of society or an embodied logic of social membership that furnishes the deep communicative structure of public life.

I propose, therefore, to set forth an explicitly Durkheimian conception of the interrelationship between our two bodies – the communicative and the physical body. The basic feature of this approach to social organization is to treat its members' categorization of bodily attitudes, functions, and relations as socially learned and socially sanctioned embodiments of the *socio-logic* of communicative bodies. How such arguments proceed is nicely illustrated in Robert Hertz's (1960) study of the right hand. So far as we can see, the resemblance between the right and left hands seem perfect. Yet, as we know, we use our hands quite differently, neglecting, avoiding, and even dishonoring the left hand, while preferring and according all sorts of privileges to the right. Each of us can imagine instances of the inequality we assign to our hands for particular purposes – as in greetings, or in wedding ceremonies. There are, of course, all sorts of variations in these practices. The whole matter may be dismissed as nothing but silly superstition or else quickly disposed of with a little knowledge of brain science. The latter settles the issue in the functional asymmetry of the brain, the dominance of the left side of the brain being responsible for the dominance of the right hand. In this case, as with so many other sociological phenomena, the competing accounts are themselves social phenomena. Curiously enough, the sneaking suspicion that we are dealing with superstition and not science is on the right track, despite its own deference toward science as the explanatory key. To put it from the other side, we may very well admit the basic phenomenon of organic asymmetry. Most people are right-handed, and relatively few are left-handed – by nature, as we say – while others seem to be ambidextrous, educable to either side. Yet these facts are not sufficient to take account of the massive social preference for the right side over the left. In short, there is a pervasive dualist symbolism to which the right and left hand are assimilated as part of the world's order:

> How could man's body, the microcosm, escape the law of polarity which governs everything? Society and the whole universe have a side which is sacred, noble and precious, and another which is profane and common: a male side, strong and active, and another, female, weak and passive; or, in two words, a right and a left side – and yet the human organism alone should be symmetrical? A moment's reflection shows us that it is an impossibility. Such an exception would not only be an inexplicable anomaly it would ruin the entire economy of the spiritual world. (Hertz, 1960: 98)

In view of the attention we have already given to the cosmic symbolism of the world's body, we can be more brief with its bearing upon the right hand. We can understand how it is that men will attribute strength and weakness, rectitude and turpitude, good fortune and evil to either side of their own bodies, as well as repeating this distribution between male and female bodies. Incidentally the injustice in these attributions lies not in the impositions of one side upon the other; each is unthinkable without the other. Justice lies in the complementarity of the gendered parts; evil resides in the disturbance of the system. It is this economy which is respected in the Last Judgment, where the Lord's raised right hand points to the heavenly abode of the elect while his lowered left hand points the path toward the hell of the damned. Therefore, the right hand is raised in prayer, the right foot enters a holy place, and the wedding ring is taken in the right hand and placed upon the left finger; and the right hand takes oaths, gives blessings, stops the traffic. In all these cases, the right hand transmits the benign and blessed life-giving and life-preserving forces of the world's own right region. In view of this symbolism, the left side, the left hand, even the political left are thought to disturb justice and goodness wherever they seek to gain predominance over the right. And, if we seem fickle in giving turns to the right and left in dances, and in politics, might it not be that we still have deep respect for the balance of good and evil in our lives?

I shall argue, starting from this analogy, that *just as we think society with our bodies so, too, we think our bodies with society*. To do so I shall rely upon various studies by Mary Douglas (1970; 1973a, b; 1975; 1978), both because they so nicely illustrate the bodily ties between individuals and institutions and because they help us to understand the relative claims of psychological and sociological analysis with respect to bodily conduct that it is otherwise tempting to consider wholly biopsychological in nature. Thus, in all societies there are curiosities of behavior which center upon a concern with bodily dirt. Sometimes it is bodily parts, or bodily functions, or whole bodies, or classes of bodies that are considered sources of either purity or pollution. We generally keep ourselves clean but give ourselves an extra special wash and brush for special occasions – for dates, interviews, funerals, or our own weddings. We are as careful to avoid our own dirt, to remove it from sight, as we are to avoid the dirt of others. Moreover, with dirt, as with so many other matters related to the body, our concerns are not nearly so physical as moral:

> If we can abstract pathogenicity and hygiene from our notion of dirt, we are left with the old definition of dirt as matter out of place. This is a very sugges- tive approach. It implies two conditions: a set of ordered relations and a con- travention of that order. Dirt, then, is never a unique, isolated event. Where there is dirt there is system. Dirt is the by-product of a systematic ordering and classification of matter, in so far as ordering involves rejecting inappropriate elements. This idea of dirt takes us straight into the field of symbolism and promises a link-up with more obviously symbolic systems of purity. (Douglas, 1970: 48)

Food in our mouths is where it should be; visible as we chew or on our chins it is disgusting. Sloppy eaters risk social and moral disapproval – the pain of being considered pigs or uncivilized. Here again, we see that the body is not just a biological entity. Eating, therefore, is not simply a matter of replacing the body's energy. To the extent that it is, eating approaches feeding – and McDonald's is a more appropriate setting for it than Maxim's , as we shall show later. Human beings have to eat, to be sure. But to receive social and moral approval, they must eat like their own kind – like members of their own race, caste, class, religion, and age group. Not – when adults – like animals, savages, heathens, and babies. In this regard, we may gain an insight into the otherwise curious provisions of the dietary rules and abominations of Leviticus as well as our own meat culture (as I will show later on):

> And the Lord spoke unto Moses and to Aaron, saying unto them,
> Speak unto the children of Israel, saying, These are the beasts which ye shall eat among all the beasts that are on earth.
> Whatsoever parteth the hoof, and is cloven-footed, and cheweth the cud among the beasts, that shall ye eat.
> Nevertheless these shall ye not eat of them that chew the cud, or of them that divide the hoof: the camel, because he cheweth the cud, but divideth not the hoof; he is unclean unto you.

And the rock badger, because he cheweth the cud, but divideth not the hoof; he is unclean unto you.

And the hare, because he cheweth the cud, but divideth not the hoof; he is unclean unto you.

And the swine, though he divide the hoof, and be clovenfooted, yet he cheweth not the cud; he is unclean to you.

Of their flesh shall ye not eat, and their carcass shall ye not touch; they are unclean to you.

These shall ye eat of all that are in the waters: whatsoever hath fins and scales in the waters, in the seas, and in the rivers, them shall ye eat.

And all that have not fins and scales in the seas, and in the rivers, of all that move in the waters, and of any living thing which is in the waters, they shall be an abomination unto you.

They shall be even an abomination unto you; ye shall not eat of their flesh, but ye shall have their carcasses in abomination.

Whatsoever hath no fins or scales in the waters, that shall be an abomination unto you.

And these are they which ye shall have in abomination among the fowls; they shall not be eaten, they are an abomination: the eagle, and the ossifrage, and the osprey,

And the kite, and falcon after its kind;

Every raven after its kind;

And the ostrich, and the night hawk, and the sea gull, and the hawk after its kind;

And the white owl, and the cormorant, and the horned owl,

And the swan, and the pelican, and the carrion eagle,

And the stork, and the heron after its kind, and the hoopoe, and the bat.

All winged insects, going upon all four, shall be an abomination unto you.

Yet these may ye eat of every winged insect that goeth upon all four, which have legs above their feet, with which to leap upon the earth;

Even these of them ye may eat: the locust after its kind, and the bald locust after its kind, and the beetle after its kind, and the grasshopper after its kind.

But all other winged insects, which have four feet, shall be an abomination unto you ...

And every creeping thing that creepeth upon the earth shall be an abomination; it shall not be eaten.

Whatsoever goeth upon the belly, and whatsoever goeth upon all four, or whatsoever hath many feet among all creeping things that creep upon the earth, them ye shall not eat; for they are an abomination.

Ye shall not make yourselves abomination with any creeping thing that creepeth, neither shall ye make yourselves unclean with them, that ye should be defiled thereby.

For I am the Lord your God: ye shall therefore sanctify yourselves, and ye shall be holy; for I am holy: neither shall ye defile yourselves with any manner of creeping that creepeth upon the earth.

For I am the Lord who bringeth you up out of the land of Egypt, to be your God; ye shall therefore be holy, for I am holy.

(Lev. 11:1–23; 41–5)

The meaning of these rules has exercised biblical scholars for some time. By and large, either the rules are considered meaningless, serving only doctrinal purposes, or else they are thought to be allegories of virtues and vices. But in either case it is difficult to see what determines the general demarcation of clean from unclean animals, even though some cases fit practical rules of hygiene. Where allegorical interpretation is pursued, it amounts to little more than pious commentary – as when Philo finds those fish with fins and scales acceptable because they symbolize endurance and self-control, while those without are swept away by the current, without resisting or lifting themselves up by prayer! Some understanding may be possible, however, if we pay attention to the repeated injunction that accompanies the various exclusions in respect of animals, childbirth, leprosy, skin disease, and sexual secretions of the body – namely the injunction to be *holy:* 'For I am the LORD who bringeth you up out of the land of Egypt, to be your God; ye shall therefore be holy for I am holy' (Lev. 11:45).

We must, then, look for the connections between holiness and the abominations. God's essential work is to create order through which men's affairs prosper – their women, livestock, and fields are kept fertile, their enemies, liars, cheats, and perverts destroyed or prevented. The holy man respects God's order and so enjoys his blessing. To infringe God's order is to run the risk of losing his blessing and suffering the consequences. Each thing in God's order must therefore respect its own kind and not risk hybridization, promiscuity and perversion:

> Thou shalt not lie with mankind, as with womankind: it is abomination. Neither shalt thou lie with any beast to defile thyself therewith; neither shall any woman stand before a beast to lie down thereto: it is confusion. (Lev. 18:22–3)

Holiness, then, consists in preserving the classes of Genesis, and it is this injunction that is basic to the laws on clean and unclean meats. To preserve the convenant between Israel and God, the land, its cattle, and its people, the Israelites are enjoined from mixing, confusing, and disordering any of the categories of the earth, waters, and heavens. As Mary Douglas shows us (Figure 2.1), a commensal order is revealed in the following schema:

1 Animals are categorized according to their degree of holiness, ranging from the abominable through those fit for the table, not the altar, to those fit for sacrifice. These degrees of holiness apply to all creatures, in the water, in the air, and on land
2 Only domesticated animals can be used as sacrificial offerings. Thus in the category of land creatures in the diagram (a), quadrupeds with parted hoofs and that chew the cud are fit for the table (b), and, from among these, domesticated herds and flocks (c) are the source for first-born offerings to the priest (d). The remaining categories represent anomalous creatures that live between two spheres or have hybrid morphological features; or else cut across all categories like the swarming, which are therefore the most abominable.
3 Denizens of the land (a) walk or hop with four legs; (b) fit for table; (c) domestic herds and flocks; (d) fit for altar; (f) abominable: insufficient criteria for (a); (g) abominable: insufficient criteria for (b); (x) abominable: swarming.

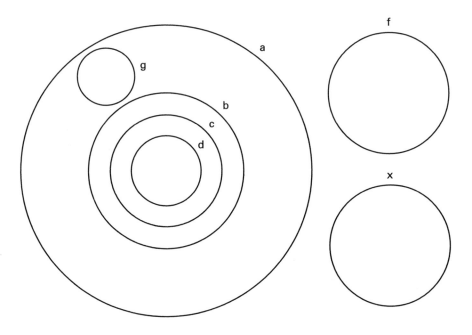

3. Denizens of the land (a) walk or hop with four legs; (b) fit for table; (c) domestic herds and flocks; (d) fit for altar; (f) abominable: insufficient criteria for (a); (g) abominable: insufficient criteria for (b); (x) abominable: swarming. Reproduced from Mary Douglas, 'Deciphering a Meal,' *Ecology in Theory and Practice*, ed. Jonathan Benthall, ©The Institute of Contemporary Arts 1972, by permission of The Institute of Contemporary Arts.

Figure 2.1   *Deciphering a meal*

We can now trace how the rules enjoining the separation of animals function to sustain the separation of the Israelites from their neighbors. The common meal identifies the Jews both to themselves and to outsiders. It constitutes a political as well as a religious boundary between Jews and non-Jews. Can we say anything more specific about these prohibitions before we consider the rest of their syntactic relations? Jean Soler (1979) argues that the Mosaic laws must be related to the account of man's food given in Genesis: 'And God said, "Behold, I have given you every herb bearing seed which is upon the face of all the earth, and every tree, in which is like fruit of a tree yielding seed; to you it shall be for food"' (Gen. 1:29).

In the first creation, paradise appears to be vegetarian. Adam is not to eat from the tree of knowledge, however. God preserves for himself immortality. He alone is the source of life. Man therefore may not take life. This difference between God and man is expressed in their respective foods. Only God may accept a living sacrifice. How then did men come to kill and eat meat? This is God's dispensation to Noah inasmuch as God saved his creation though he recognized its violence and murder. The third covenant, between

God and Moses, separates the Hebrews from the rest of humankind; and it is here that we find the separations (cuts) of the Sabbath, circumcision, and the clean and unclean animals, which together constitute a symbolic system functioning to preserve Jewish religious and political identity. In particular, the taboo against blood is reinforced, so that the priest must make a peace offering of the blood of the sacrificial animal to appease God for the act of slaughter. In turn, the animals appropriate for the table and the altar are herbivorous rather than carnivorous, as though the animals themselves observed the injunction against slaughter, at least in the first Genesis account: 'And to every beast of the earth, and to every foul of the air, and to everything that creepeth upon the earth, wherein there is life, I have given every green herb for food' (Gen. 1:30).

Soler argues, therefore, that it is the 'hoofed foot' which separates the herbivorous animals from the clawed predators on land and in the air. It remains to explain why clean animals have two further predicates, namely a 'cloven hoof' and that they 'chew the cud'. The effect of the latter is to exclude pigs, which, though they have hoofed feet and are herbivorous, are also carnivorous. There remains some uncertainty about wild herbivorous animals, and therefore the 'cloven hoof' is stressed, even though that rule eliminates from the category of clean animals such borderline cases of domestication as the camel, hare, horse, and ass, which are also herbivorous. Even so, clean domesticated animals must be perfect of their kind to be sacrificed. No animal – or person – with a blemish may participate in the holy sacrifice. By the same logic of wholeness, or of identity and holiness, nothing may be mixed in the kitchen or in bed that confuses the order of things:

> This no doubt explains the Bible's most mysterious prohibition: 'You shall not boil a kid in its mother's milk' (Exod. 23:19 and 34:26; Deut. 14:21). These words must be taken quite literally. They concern a mother and her young. They can be translated as: you shall not put a mother and her son in the same pot, any more than into the same bed. Here as elsewhere, it is a matter of upholding the separation between two classes or two types of relationships. To abolish distinction by means of a sexual or culinary act is to subvert the order of the world. Everyone belongs to one species only, one people, one sex, one category. And in the same manner, everyone has only one God: 'See now that I, even I, am he, and there is no God beside me' (Deut. 32:39). The keystone of this order is the principle of identity, instituted as the law of every being. (Soler, 1979: 30)

Let us return to the analysis offered by Mary Douglas. We can see how the purity of the categories is metonymically reproduced in the purity of persons and animals. The Jews and their animals are separated and tied to one another through the rituals of purity in the same way that the Jews are separated from other people and their animals. Thus the first-born son and the first-born of the herds and flocks are equally consecrated to divine service: a patriarchal mark that sets the people and its animals apart from other peoples and animals. As the first-born of the Israelites, the Levites are judges of their purity and among the Levites themselves only those without blemish may enter the Holy of Holies – the perfectly bounded sanctuary between God and man. The Jewish dietary rules, therefore, may be regarded as what Vico would call a 'severe poem', dedicated to the political preservation of a people whose holiness is the mark of their will to survive.

Can we say more as to why the Jews (and Islamites) don't eat pork? There are in fact further questions to be settled with respect to the taxonomic status of the pig – as well as a wholly different approach to pigs as protein. Consider once again Leviticus 11:1–8. The pig is an unclean animal – like the hare, the hyrax, and the camel, it is an abomination. Because they do not have both cloven hoofs and the capacity to chew the cud, these animals are not clean. The pig, moreover, is the only land animal with cloven hoofs that does not chew the cud. Under pressure from critics (Bulmer, 1967; Tambiah, 1969; Douglas, 1973). Douglas came to see that, since anomalies may be either abominated or revered, animal taxonomies are best understood in relation to social rules about residence and marriage. Following Durkheim, we can expect the boundaries of natural classifications to be as permeable or impermeable as the boundaries of the social systems to which they belong. Social boundaries are regulated by (among other things) the rules for marriage – the rules of exogamy and incest avoidance – whose effect is to admit strangers to the circle of kinsman. The Israelites had no prohibition against first-cousin marriages, which meant that in-marrying was preferred to marriage alliances either with other lineages or tribes among the Israelites or with foreigners. Surrounded by enemies, the Jews were particularly vexed by the problem of the stranger, especially since some, like the Samaritans, also claimed to be Israelites. The Jews could marry prisoners of war, and obviously they had absorbed the Canaanites. The risk taken in marrying strangers entailed the risk of eating their food, and the pig was more likely to be sacrificed for a wedding than the camel or hare. Therefore in the same way that the Jews insisted upon their historical identity they also insisted upon the identity of Jahweh and of their own classes of clean and unclean animals: 'It would seem that whenever a people are aware of encroachment and danger, dietary rules controlling what goes into the body would serve as a vivid analogy of the corpus of their cultural categories at risk' (Douglas, 1975: 272).

Here, then, we have a fine example of the socio-logic of incorporation that underlies the concept of the body politic, to the general history of which we shall turn in the next chapter. Before doing so, however, we should consider a more directly materialist challenge to Douglas's political account of pig taxonomy and political history. Among a number of essays directly or indirectly responding to Douglas that have raised quite a storm are Marvin Harris's speculations on the love/hatred of the pig prevalent among Jews and Moslems, excluding them from the succulence of roast pig celebrated in Lamb's essay, as well as depriving them from an extremely efficient protein processor:

The pig taboo recurs throughout the entire vast zone of Old World pastoral nomadism – from North Africa across the Middle East and Central Asia. But in

China, South East Asia, Indonesia and Melanesia the pig was and still is a much-used source of dietary proteins and fats, as it is in modern Europe and the Western Hemisphere. The fact that the pig was tabooed in the great pastoral zones of the Old World and in several of the river valleys bordering these zones suggests that the Biblical taboos must be seen as an adaptive response valuable over a wide area in relation to recurrent ecological shifts brought about by the intensification and depletions associated with the rise of ancient states and empires. (Harris, 1978: 203–4)

Harris argues that with the rise of the ancient states, and the larger populations they required, it was necessary to shift from raising pigs, sheep, goats, and cattle primarily for meat and to put more land under the plough for wheat, barley and other plant crops, which have roughly ten times greater calorie return than the animal sources gained by the same expenditure. In short, Harris claims, there was a decision to raise and feed people on plant crops rather than raise and feed meat-producing animals for a smaller return. In addition, the use of domesticated animals changed; instead of being a meat source of proteins, they became a milk-based protein source. While this particular strategy may have been rational, Harris claims that with respect to the consumption of basic amino acids, the shift from meat to plant foods resulted in a diminishing standard of nutrition, health, and vigor. Furthermore, he claims that because the pig has no use other than meat-protein production, even though it yields two or three times as many calories as cattle or chickens, it was the first domestic species to become too expensive to raise and thus to incur religious taboo. This change in the nutritional status of the pig resulted in large part from a shift in the ratio of grassland to forest, where the pig finds the kind of tubers, roots, fruits, and nuts it most efficiently converts to meat. Above all, it finds in the forest the shade it needs, since pigs, Harris says, cannot regulate their body temperature by sweating. Actually, pigs sweat like pigs by wallowing (Baldwin, 1974). When the Israelites arrived in Palestine, they rapidly converted the forests in the Judaean and Samaritan hills to pasture land. Consequently pig raising became much more expensive, however tempting. Hence the taboos upon the pig as an unclean animal reinforced the need to avoid its domestication in large numbers that would have to be fed on grain supplements that could more efficiently be used for human consumption.

Harris is aware that there is a certain redundancy in this materialist account. If humans are by nature economists, why in the face of the inefficiency of pig production would they be tempted to raise pigs? Why would the poor Irish need meatless Fridays (Douglas, 1973: 59–76) when they could easily see that fish was a cheaper source of protein? He nevertheless argues that the cost/benefit principle applied equally well to the rest of the unclean animals insofar as they were both in short supply and obtainable only by hunting. Since pastoralists were not likely to be good at hunting or fishing and would get little meat from such efforts, the religious taboos contained in Leviticus prove that its authors were able economists rather than poor doctors or classificatory maniacs. Rather than treating the pig taboo in terms of peculiarly Israelite concerns with taxonomy and religious identity, Harris concludes that it, and similar curiosities, can be understood only as an economic response to a shifting food environment:

> The link between the depletion of animal proteins on the one hand, and the practice of human sacrifice and cannibalism, the evolution of ecclesiastical redistributive feasting, and the tabooing of the flesh of certain animals on the other, demonstrates the unmistakable causal priority of material costs and benefits over spiritual beliefs – not necessarily for all time, but almost certainly for the cases in question. (Harris, 1978: 154)

I cannot close off this controversy without bringing it into the orbit of the structuralist approach to the categorization of human beings, animals, and food. I do so in only the simplest fashion and more with a view to providing Harris's opponent, Marshall Sahlins (1976), with a voice than to entering into the labyrinths of Lévi-Strauss's thought (Leach, 1970). It is tempting to see in Harris's thesis a strong version of the materialist arguments that might characterize a Marxist anthropology. Yet it is in the name of a Marxist cultural anthropology that Sahlins rejects Harris's reduction of practical reason to the sheerest calculation. We are concerned with people's relation to their food. It might be thought that such a relation is simply bioeconomic. Humans need a diet that will more than replace the energy they expend in procuring it. That is the sole significance of food and eating. Yet people seem to distinguish themselves from animals in that we *eat* whereas animals *feed*. In view of the largely learned and socially organized classification of foods considered edible and inedible, together with elaborate codes for their preparation and serving, it seems unlikely that Harris's cost benefit theorem can be the complete explanation. Indeed, utilitarianism of any sort is generally a poor guide to what it is consumers pursue in making their lives longer, more beautiful, sexy and self-assured. Utilitarianism or materialism is rather the form of consciousness through which bourgeois society hides from itself its nonrational economy, as we shall see in Chapter 4.

The symbolic values that circulate in both the production and the consumption sectors of the economy cannot be reduced to a pragmatic logic of efficiency except at the cost of hiding from ourselves the larger cultural economy in which we labor and consume. To show the truth of this proposition, Sahlins offers his own account (1976) of the cultural preferences underlying American food habits, drawing upon work of Douglas, Edmund Leach and Lévi-Strauss (1970) that we have already considered in its bare essentials. Thus meat is the center of the American meal. Steak in particular is a man's food. It is American, recalling the hard work of ranching, the sagas of cowboys and Indians, and a way of life for men halfway between the nomad and the townsman. Americans eat meat. They eat steaks, hamburgers, pork, and ham; but they do not eat horses and dogs. Unlike the French, they do not to any extent even feed horses to dogs. Rather, they go to elaborate lengths to feed dogs and cats like themselves, though perhaps assigning to their pets more entrails or offal than their owners care for. How are we to explain such curiosities? Once again, we can entertain rival explanations. Americans, it will be said, are the world's busiest people. They therefore collectively use and produce enormous quantities of energy ranging from hydroelectricity to oil and, of course, proteins on the individual level. The American body is an energy factory producing health, strength, youth, smiles, sex, and satisfaction. Naturally the American diet is geared to all this. Notwithstanding the malnutritional aspects of fast food chains, *fast food is the totemic American food*. In other words, Americans eat high on the hog; and when they stop to look around, they view those who don't as either poor, unsuccessful, lazy, or sick, or else as food freaks opting out of the mainstream, munching on vegetarian diets and nonaggressive philosophies of life. Meat, the mainstay of the American way of life, is identical with American strength and industriousness.

Following Leach (1964), let us look at how the domesticated animal series – cattle, pigs, horses, dogs, regarded as a chain of decreasing edibility – might be mapped against a series of social relations representing decreasing degrees of community/commensality. Thus it is noticeable that there are fairly strong distinctions between edible and inedible animals, and similarly within the edible category – cattle and pork – a strong distinction between the 'meat' and the 'innards' of the animals. In other words, Americans observe a food taboo with respect to horses and dogs and are squeamish, at least, about innards. Why do they think their food this way? In accordance with Leach's argument, we may notice that the food taboo correlates with the kinship series insofar as horses and dogs share human company, have names, are friends, and can be loved. Cattle and pigs are less human in this respect. Eating the meat of these animals is eating less of the quintessential animal than eating its innards, again preserving the boundary between humans and animals despite the daily necessity of infringing it. This boundary is in turn reproduced socioeconomically in that the higher classes can afford more steak than the lower; the poorer, especially blacks, being driven to 'cheaper cuts' and, of course, to innards.

Can we radically rethink society with our bodies? Or are we caught in categorical systems that think us? To conclude, I would like to take another look at the symbolic status of meat in the American economy. It is generally thought that Americans are among the best fed people in the world. It is part of this conventional wisdom that American charity is typically disbursed in the form of food and grain to starving people elsewhere. Actually American dairy dumping and the protein myth have considerable negative transnational effects upon weaker agricultural societies (Crawford and Rivers, 1975). In reality, the United States is no more self-sufficient in food than in any other enterprise on which the American economy prides itself. The terrible truth is that the United States shares in the Western world's net importation of proteins from the undernourished (and frequently starving) 'Third World':

Through oil seeds (peanuts, palm kernels, copra, etc.), oilseed products, and fish meal, the Western world is currently acquiring from the hungry world one million metric tons more protein than is delivered to the hungry world through grains. In other words, the Western world is exchanging approximately 3 million metric tons of cereal protein for 4 million metric tons of other proteins which are all superior in nutritive aspects. (Borgstrom, 1973: 64)

What is even more astonishing is the nature of the production process that supplies the American passion for meat as a central dish, whether at home, in restaurants, or in fast food chains. The cycle begins with the enormously increased productivity of American grains as a result of genetic seed improvements and the use of fertilizers and pesticides. We ignore the health hazards resulting from these procedures, though they bear, of course, on the issues to be considered in the later chapter on medical bodies. Americans ingeniously give grain away, waste food, and dump dairy products abroad, but nothing disposes of as much American grain as the American steer. In the conversion of plant protein to animal protein, the average steer requires sixteen pounds of grain per pound of meat on the table, hogs require six, turkeys four, chickens three, and milk one per pint. Or, to look at the matter the other way around, an acre of cereals yields five times more protein than an acre given to meat production; an acre of beans, peas, or lentils is ten times more efficient, and leafy vegetables fifteen times in producing protein. The American steer is a protein factory in reverse! Furthermore, to keep meat enshrined in the American food market it is necessary to maintain the feedlot operation – the forced feeding of grains, soybeans, milk products, fish meal, wheat germ under assembly line conditions that also require the introduction of hormones and antibiotics – with incidental health risks to American consumers and the certain risk of starvation to millions elsewhere in the world. The author of *Diet for a Small Planet* notes:

If we exclude dairy cows, the average conversion ratio for U.S. livestock is 7 pounds of grain and soy feed to produce one pound of edible meat. (Note that this figure is an *average* of relatively high [chicken] and low [steer] efficiency converters.) According to this estimate, of the 140 million tons of grain and soy we fed to our beef cattle, poultry and hogs in 1971, *one-seventh*, or only 20 million tons, was returned to us in meat. *The rest, almost 118 million tons of grain and soy, became unaccessible for human consumption.* Although we lead the world in exports of grain and soy, this incredible volume 'lost' through livestock was twice the level of our current exports. It is enough to provide every single human being on earth with more than a cup of cooked grain each day of the year! (Lappé, 1975: 13–14)

Americans get rich by making America a market that is rich. America's wealth is not produced. It is desired. Wealth and poverty are effects of greater or lesser desire which is a matter of character but not of class. America is governed by socially structured *anomie*, that is, by the limitlessness of its desire. In such a society, all objects are constructed to meet the denial of scarcity. The result is that shoddy rules in the material order while mortification rules in the spiritual order. Americans are destined to disappointment rather than disaffection. McDonald's is the perfect venue for this daily experience. Here the customer is a self-serving sovereign whose taste dictates every movement within a menu designed to eject him or her and his or her family as fast as possible.

Thus the artful McDonald's consumer is pitted from the moment s/he leaves the counter against food that is already beginning to turn cold and to decompose (nor can it be reheated). A decision must be made to swallow fast – facilitated by meat and potatoes that in any case need no biting or chewing, and by condiments that soften them up further. McFood is fast because only you can slow it down. Since you serve yourself – only you are responsible for how and what you eat. Once you have paid for McMeal, you are on your own. You serve the food; you seat yourself; you pace your meal; you clean up the remains:

McCommunion

1 Get in line.
2 Look up to the menu.
3 Order food and drink and extra condiments.
4 Pay when order is registered.
5 Serve yourself napkins, straws and implements (no cutlery).
6 Seat yourself.
7 Eat and Drink.
8 Clean away after yourself – Thank you.
9 Exit.
10 Steps (5–8) can be saved in Drive-Away and (5–6) in Drive-In, where the automobile *is* the restaurant.

At McDonald's the family escapes from itself to celebrate a meal it has not cooked, a meal about which nothing need be said that has not already been said and that can be forgotten the minute it is over – give and take a little indigestion, unless one is quite young. The organized informality of McDonald's is particularly important since it pre-empts criticism while nevertheless invoking it as suggestions for improved service. As in every confidence game, the onus is on the victim to change the game!

Americans are unsure whether America is built upon individuals or upon families. In practice, each covers for the other – and the same is true of individual and corporate relations. The American ideology phrases institutions as nothing but a set of individuals while promoting the individual as America's greatest institution (O'Neill, 1993). This encourages Americans to regard themselves as more alike than not, however unequal their corporate institutions render them. Since every society celebrates itself as a commensal order, it must eat itself – contradictions and all (Figure 2.2).

The ideological construction of the Average American services industry and democracy so that mass-produced commodities reproduce the American who consumes them. Cars, cokes and burgers are the ideal material carriers

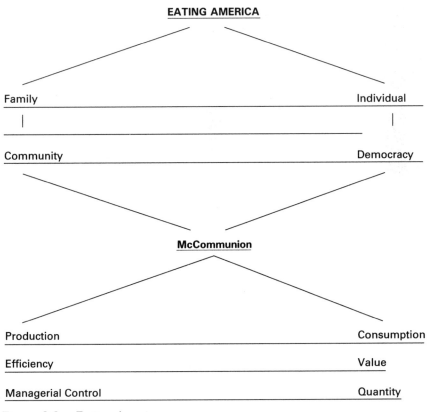

Figure 2.2   *Eating America*

of American ideology of efficiency, control, value, quantity, profit and convenience. Because American families lack the time to be families, they also lack the time to be members of communities. McDonald's is happy to declare itself a community agent. Because Americans are not sure how much change they can stand, McDonald's is happy to reassure Americans that nothing changes at McDonald's because it is timelessly devoted to the primordial values of food, folk and good clean fun. Because Americans have little time for their children, McDonald's happily offers them a haven, a treasure house of birthday memories across the generations.

We are, then, what we do or do not eat; and the same may be said of society. Our bodies are social in almost any way we care to think, and yet it is our bodies we claim from society as our most intimate and private possession. In a world where multitudes starve and others suffer from obesity still others pin to themselves 'edibaubles', rings, pins, necklaces, and earrings of plastic junk-food shapes, hamburgers, hot dogs, and apple pie. Meantime, cookbooks and gourmet food guides continue to proliferate what has been called 'gastro-porn' (Cockburn, 1977), whisking the urban aesthete into pastorales of fresh fruit and vegetables, blending New York and Provence, mixing morals and madness, economy and extravagance, all in a world of vicarious sensations whose only rival appears to be that of the sex manuals, whose metaphors are equally gastronomic. In this chapter, I have tried to show how two social orders, one archaic, the other industrial, each meat-minded, nevertheless connect to different orders of political economy and religion. In the case of biblical Judaism, religion and politics confirm the will to survive celebrated in a holy meal. In North America, the totemic meal confirms industriousness celebrated in ever faster foods. I have argued that we should rethink our meat culture in the light of a sustainable world food economy. We must also foster a civic intelligence about our health habits in respect of the rest of our food as it passes from the farm, through the factory store, home, and restaurant. By now there is a great deal of concern over the health hazards genetically manufactured into our food chain. Everyone must be made aware of this mutation. Our families and schools as well as the media must educate children, youth, and new families in these issues. The task cannot be left to the goodwill of the food corporations geared to the 'family' in the fast lane. We must insist, then, that *the family should be a thinking body*, whose common sense should be fostered in any healthy community and by any practical means. As this book proceeds, I shall formulate further propositions aimed at interceding on behalf of the civic function of a familied intelligence.

3

The Body Politic

Every political community has to find a symbolic expression of its beliefs concerning the sources, sustenance and potential threats to the orderly conduct of its members. Thus the imagery of the *body politic* recurs in our reflections on the nature of order and disorder in the human community. From the plebeian secession from Rome to the street politics of the 1960s and today's antinuclear war and global trade protests, the human body has provided the language and the very text of political protest against, and confrontation with, the agencies that administer our inhumanity. This rhetorical conception of the body politic for which I shall argue differs from the rhetoric of the administrative and therapeutic sciences in that it aspires to enhance *the communicative competence of civic democracy*. The logic of calculative rationality increasingly dominates the production and maintenance of social order, making alternative conceptions of society seem utopian and irrational. However, the repressive functions of administrative rationality have inevitably led its critics to a search for a new political symbolism, a search whose reasonableness may be conveyed through an analysis of the classical concept of the body politic. The body politic is the fundamental structure of our political life. It provides the grounds of ultimate appeal in times of deep institutional crisis, of hunger, war and ecological damage. Our appeal to the socio-logic of the body seeks to re-embed the now hegemonic technological and bureaucratic knowledge in the common-sense *bioknowledge* of persons and families whose civic lives are otherwise administered by the modern corporate economy and its therapeutic state. The urgency of this issue will be seen in Chapter 5 when we consider the technologies of medicalized power that characterize the therapeutic state.

Leonard Barkan (1975: 62) has suggested that we can trace roughly three stages in the development of the anthropomorphic image of the universe and society:

1 *Simple anthropomorphism*: This is the stage we have called the world's body. As Vico pointed out, early humans had nothing else but their bodies with which to think the cosmos and society.
2 *The organic cosmos*: in this stage the body imagery in thinking the universe and society has become abstract, its puzzles are explored. Here important elements of ancient and medieval philosophical, cosmological and theo-political thought are bequeathed to us, as we shall see further in this chapter, which also explores the next stage.

3   *The renewal of the body politic*: From time to time the imagery of the human body is again made sharp to reassert the human shape of human beings where they are threatened by social and political forces directed at administering men and women as things or automata. Here, then, we may speak of *civic anthropomorphism*, and I shall develop this insight in an effort to rethink the body politic in response to the dilemmas of everyday life in the modern administrative state with its therapeutic apparatus.

We shall first review the legacy of classical and medieval thought on the body politic. In *The Republic*, Book II, Plato could approach the nature of the *polis* only by looking for the integrative principle that made it more than a physical or natural collection. Thus, while the human body places men and women in a natural collection, it is nevertheless true that social and political life brings them together in virtue of some principle higher than natural necessity, inasmuch as men and women are also rational and moral beings. Thus, the true *polis* arises out of a 'first city' that is, as it were, merely *the body writ large*. The first city is constituted in terms of a system of exchange in wants and needs which unites men and women collectively, just as the various needs of their bodies drive them to maintain their individual bioconstitutions. In this first city, health and harmony are achieved through the coordination of the arts of trade and commerce, just as the health of the body consists in the satisfaction of its various members. It turns out, however, that the first city becomes feverish in the search for luxuries, engages in war, and consequently needs to be reorganized through the inclusion of a class of guardians, whose proper education further requires a class of philosophers with insight into the true health of the *polis*. Although the true health of the body is nothing more than what it was before it became sick, the art of its restoration has no counterpart in nature. The work of the physician and, by analogy the work of the political philosopher, is the work of civic reason. Insight into the true object of that work may be gained by treating the *polis* as a soul writ large, though I am unable to pursue this line any further.

Perhaps the most famous account of the revolutionary body politic is that given by Menenius Agrippa in his effort to avoid the plebeian secession at a critical stage in Rome's history:

> Long ago when the members of the human body did not, as now they do, agree together, but had each its own thoughts and the words to express them in, the other parts resented the fact that they should have the worry and trouble of providing everything for the belly, which remained idle, surrounded by its ministers, with nothing to do but enjoy the pleasant things they gave it. So the discontented members plotted together that the hand should carry no food to the mouth, that the mouth should take nothing that was offered it, and that the teeth should accept nothing to chew. But alas! while they sought in their resentment to subdue the belly by starvation, they themselves and the whole body wasted away to nothing. By this it was apparent that the belly, too, has no mean service to perform: it receives food, indeed; but it also nourishes in its turn the other members, giving back to all parts of the body, through all its

veins, the blood it has made by the process of digestion; and upon this blood our life and our health depend. (Livy, 1960: 141–2)

The imagery of the body politic continued to be exploited throughout the ancient and medieval period. Aristotle, Cicero, Seneca, and numerous other writers drawing upon them repeated the tropes of harmony, balance, fever, and disproportion as principal figures of political thought. A major elaboration upon these figures occurs in Saint Paul's doctrine of the *mystical body* in which the unity in difference that sustains the members of the human body is appealed to as the basis for the charismatic unity of the members of a Christian society where each exercises his talents on behalf of the others, and always as a gift of God rather than as his own property. The sublimity of the Christian conception of unity in difference is marvelously contained in the circular figures of Christ's body (Figure 3.1), which simultaneously contains the tree of life, abstracting and protecting the intimacy of its members.

Here, through these two intimate figures, the circle and the tree, we enter the boundless space of God, yet proportioned to the incarnate Christ-Man. Thus Saint Paul depicted the body as a *community of talents*:

Now there are diversities of gifts, but the same Spirit.
And there are differences of administrations, but the same Lord.
And there are diversities of operations, but it is the same God who worketh all in all.
But the manifestation of the Spirit is given to every man to profit...
For as the body is one, and hath many members, and all the members of that one body, being many are one body, so also is Christ. For by one Spirit were we all baptized into one body, whether we be Jews or Greeks, whether we be bond or free; and have been all made to drink into one Spirit.
For the body is not one member, but many.
If the foot shall say, Because I am not the hand, I am not of the body; is it, therefore, not of the body?
And if the ear shall say Because I am not the eye, I am not of the body; is it, therefore, not of the body?
If the whole body were an eye, where were the hearing? If the whole were hearing, where were the smelling?
But now hath God set the members, every one of them, in the body as it hath pleased him.
And if they were all one member, where were the body?
But now are they many members, yet but one body.
And the eye cannot say unto the hand, 1 have no need of thee; nor again the head to the feet, I have no need of you.
Nay, much more those members of the body which seem to be more feeble, are necessary:
And those members of the body, which we think to be less honorable, upon these we bestow more abundant honor; and our uncomely parts have more abundant comeliness.
For our comely parts have no need, but God hath tempered the body together, having given more abundant honor to that part which lacked,
That there should be no schism in the body, but that the members should have the same care one for another.
And whether one member suffer, all the members suffer with it; or one member be honored, all the members rejoice with it. (1 Cor. 12:4–26)

4. Manuscript illumination, Christ, C. 1341. Reproduced with the permission of the publisher from Alžběta Güntheroná and Ján Mišianik, *Illuminierte Handschriften aus der Slowakei* (Prague: Artia).

Figure 3.1   *Christ figure*

One of the most remarkable developments in the imagery of the body politic occurred in the fusion of certain doctrines of high medieval political theology with the legal fiction of the king's two bodies – the *body natural* and the *body politic*:

> The King has two Capacities, for he has two Bodies, the one whereof is a Body natural, consisting of natural Members as every other Man has, and in this he is subject to Passions and Death as other Men are; the other is a Body politic, and the Members thereof are his Subjects, and he and his Subjects together compose the Corporation, as Southcote said, and he is incorporated with them,

and they with him, and he is the Head, and they are the members, and he has the sole Government of them; and this Body is not subject to Passions as the other is, nor to Death, for as to this Body the King never dies, and his natural Death is not called in our Law (as Harper said), the Death of the King, but the Demise of the King, not signifying by the Word (Demise) that the Body politic of the King is dead, but that there is a Separation of the two Bodies, and that the Body politic is transferred and conveyed over from the Body natural now dead, or now removed from the Dignity royal, to another Body natural. So that it Signifies a Removal of the Body politic of the King of this Realm from one Body natural to another. (Kantorowicz, 1957: 13)

The fiction of the king's two bodies, as is evident from a closer look at the wording of the preceding passage, draws upon the corporate doctrine of the Roman church elaborated in Carolingian times from sources in Saint Paul (Robinson, 1952). Roughly what happened is that the mystical body of Christ (the Eucharist) and the body of Christ (the church and the faithful on earth throughout history) merged in response to controversy over the real presence of Christ in the Eucharist. Thus the Eucharist became simply *corpus christi* (formerly Christian society) and the church became *corpus mysticum*, formerly the term for the Eucharist. So at the very time when the church was beginning to achieve recognition as a secular power among other secular legal and political institutions, it thereby offered to these institutions the distinction between Christ's natural body and his spiritual or ecclesiastical body:

> it had been the custom to talk about the Church as the 'mystical body of Christ' (*corpus corpus Christi mysticum*) which sacramentally alone makes sense. Now, however, the Church, which had been the mystical body of Christ, became a mystical body in its own right. That is, the Church organism became a 'mystical body' in an almost juristic sense: a mystical corporation. The change in terminology was not haphazardly introduced. It signified just another step in the direction of allowing the clerical corporational institution of the *corpus ecclesiae iuridicum* to coincide with the *corpus ecclesiae mysticum* and thereby to 'secularize' the notion of 'mystical body'. (Kantorowicz, 1957: 201)

Moreover, this shift in terminology made it easier for the pope to be the political head of the church's secular body politic than of the Eucharistic body of the church. By the same token, the terminology was in place for the juridical appropriation by the strictly secular body politic of the spiritual and transcendental predicates of the mystical body. It remained for the jurists to work out the doctrines of the corporate continuity of the state. In particular, there was the problem of furnishing the king with two bodies so that his natural 'demise' could be survived by his body politic. We cannot follow the arguments whereby further distinctions were elaborated concerning the public and private capacities of the king, the inalienable sovereignty of the people, and the relative claims of natural and positive law. What I want to stress is that medieval corporate theory was never tempted to the later-nineteenth-century fictions of the organic or totalitarian state. The medieval tradition, on the contrary, split the two sovereignties of the state and the individual. This tradition, certain features of which I argue below for reviving, has always resisted any fiction of the state as a higher spiritual entity – indeed, it might even underwrite the call for revolution as we shall show.

During the Renaissance, political thinkers continued to employ body imagery as a guide to thinking the relation between the head of the state and its members (Archambault, 1967). Thus it was conceivable to Aeneas Sylvius when he wrote his *De ortu et auctoritate imperie romani* (1466), a treatise on the origins and authority of Roman rule, that the prince's head might be sacrificed like a hand or a foot, if it saved the life of the body politic. It was axiomatic to this way of thinking that the body had a prior claim to life over its members: herein lay also the possibility of defending lies, deception, and injustice toward individuals if it served the corporate body. Of course, Aeneas Sylvius (later Pope Pius II) could hardly have envisaged anything salutary in a decapitated state. Yet for later regicides this issue might have been more difficult without the doctrine of the king's two bodies, the one secular and disposable, the other spiritual and hence not biodegradable. How the body image functioned with respect to the possibility of an acephalous state is nicely portrayed in Sir John Fortescue's defense of a moderate monarchy, written in the years from 1468 to 1471:

> Saint Augustine, in the 19th book of the *De Civitate Dei*, chapter 23, said that *A people is a body of men united by consent of law and by community of interest.* But such a people does not deserve to be called a body whilst it is acephalous, i.e., without a head. Because, just as in natural bodies, what is left over after decapitation is not a body, but is what we call a trunk, so in bodies politic a community without a head is not by any means a body. Hence Aristotle in the first book of the *Politics* said that *Whensoever one body is constituted out of many, one will rule, and the others be ruled.* So a people wishing to erect itself into a kingdom or any other body politic must always set up one man for the government of all that body who, by analogy with a kingdom, is, from 'regendo', usually called a king. As in this way the physical body grows out of the embryo, regulated by one head, so the kingdom issues from the people, and exists as a body mystical, governed by one man as head. And just as in the body natural, as Aristotle said, the heart is the source of life, having in itself the blood which it transmits to all the members thereof, whereby they are quickened and live, so in the body politic the will of the people is the source of life, having in it the blood, namely, political forethought for the interest of the people, which it transmits to the head and all the members of the body by which the body is maintained and quickened. (Fortescue, 1942: 31)

Thus between Aeneas Sylvius and Sir John Fortescue we see an interesting alternation. If the prestige of the head over the heart and stomach is preserved, the body politic leans toward authority; whereas if the vital services of the stomach or the heart are emphasized, it leans toward moderate monarchy (it would be wrong to speak of democracy in the latter case, since no one favored a body with many heads!) To vary the image just slightly, the prince as the physician of the body politic may be considered the source of the troubles from which his patients suffer and more likely to heal them by forebearing the exercise of his crude medicine. Such was the opinion of Montaigne, whose skepticism with regard to medicine was even greater than it was toward philosophy:

> The preservation of states is a thing that probably surpasses our understanding. As Plato says, a civil government is a powerful thing and hard to dissolve. It often holds out against mortal internal disease, against the mischief of unjust laws, against tyranny against the excesses and ignorance of the magistrates and the licence and sedition of the people. (Montaigne 1965: 732–3)

However, where the prince is seen as a philosophical doctor, as by Budé or Erasmus, then we have a more trusting view of his ministrations than otherwise seems justified by princely ignorance and corruption. In either case, the body politic does well to be sturdy, evenly balanced and not subject to extremes of temperament and wealth if it is to survive the ministrations of its rulers. Thus, Machiavelli (1950) also based his rude political advice upon the capacity of the 'mixed' body to survive change and destruction and to renew itself. Generally, however, the body image served the interests of limited monarchy, as well expressed once again by Sir John Fortescue:

> The law, indeed, by which a group of men is made into a people, resembles the nerves of the body physical, for, just as the body is held together by the nerves, so this body mystical is bound together and united into one by the law, which is derived from the word '*ligando*', and the members and bones of this body, which signify the solid basis of truth by which the community is sustained, preserve their rights through the law, as the body natural does through the nerves. And just as the head of the body physical is unable to change its nerves, or to deny its members proper strength and due nourishment of blood, so a king who is head of the body politic is unable to change the laws of that body, or to deprive that same people of their own substance uninvited or against their wills. You have here, prince, the form of the institution of the political kingdom, whence you can estimate the power that the king can exercise in respect of the law and the subjects, and their bodies and goods, and he has power to this end issuing from the people, so that it is not permissible for him to rule his people with any other power. (Fortescue, 1942: 33)

The fraternal political romance that runs from the French Revolution through to the Russian Revolution and its Left offspring of today also draws upon the subversive potential of the patriarchal family once its women and children become political actors in their own right: 'The new forms of social organization did not simply incarnate the power of the father; they instituted a fragile, unstable, constantly shifting equilibrium between the individual and the family. There remained the vivid imagery of the father's cut-off head' (Hunt, 1992: 191).

With these considerations in mind, I hope to avoid any suggestion that in the following attempt to revive certain features of the ancient and medieval conception of the body politic (Gierke, 1958) I am reversing the liberal individualist tradition in favor of an organicist and totalitarian conception of political life. Rather, as I see it, it is precisely because the modern liberal administrative state has succumbed to 'organization' that we find ourselves trying to rethink the body politic. Admittedly, trying to revive the imagery of the body politic is a huge challenge to the political imagination. The weight of political rhetoric is all in the other direction. That is to say, political discourse is increasingly shaped to the legitimation needs of the administrative state and its agenda for public and private allocations of socioeconomic goods and services (Habermas, 1975). To make possible the state's intervention in major domains of social and economic life, it is necessary to treat the administration of these areas as the task of expert technical sciences, whose professional practice requires a client- or patient-model of citizenry. Thus, as Habermas (1975: 36) has argued, we find that the administrative state requires the depoliticization of the public realm, and brings that about by fostering simultaneously (1) *civil privatism*: the pursuit of consumption, leisure, and careers in exchange for political abstinence; (2) *public depoliticization*: the ideological justification of (1) by means of elitist theories of the democratic process and by technocratic accounting procedures that rationalize administrative power. These two strategies encourage a species of neo-individualism divorced from any critical and public intelligence. This process is compounded by the dependency of the liberal welfare state upon the multinational/global corporate agenda. Furthermore, global corporations can presume an *ex post facto* ratification of their allocation of resources between private and public goods and services. Thus, the liberal state underwrites the gap between the promise and the actual performance of the market by means of its own economic activities, even while it is claiming that these restore a rational social agenda. These strategies require a technical style of political discourse to which the imagery of the body politic is foreign.

Yet the fact is that men and women, and especially many young people, are unhappy with the administration of their lives. They perceive this dissatisfaction not simply as resulting from economic exploitation but also as a state of pervasive *linguistic alienation* from the bureaucratic and administrative discourse of the experts who function on behalf of the state, schools, hospitals, and social agencies. The rationalization of the administered society requires that political discourse be problem-specific and subject to decisionistic or calculative reasoning. In turn, the very scientificity of the language and reportage of the social sciences contribute to the administrative effort to manage behavior and institutions according to standards of maximum efficiency. The latter, however, are ill suited for dealing with the daily experience of unemployment, ignorance, and teenage suicide and pregnancies which fall upon families, churches, and local agencies that must cope as best they can. Moreover, the administered society's ability by and large to command allegiance in exchange for granting participation in goods and services reduces political participation to the demand for 'information' about irreversible events, disapproval of which we have a residual right to express in elections when turn-out is often precarious. The combined effect of these processes upon the communicative competence of citizens, families, churches, and local communities is that discourse about the ideal values of political, economic, and social life is marginalized and alienated as talk lacking any rational or decisionistic grammar.

Elsewhere, I have tried to show that street antics, rock music, and the dirty-speech movement of the 1960s (and the global protests against the

World Trade Organization at the turn of this century) despite their apparently irrational and destructive appearance (aggravated by media focus on incidents of property damage, stone throwing), represent real expressions of the communicative competence of populations responding to global corporate and military domination (O'Neill, 1972; 2002). At first sight, from the participants' speech, dress, and improvised resources, these movements appear to be impoverished attempts to confront the legitimacy of the corporate, economic, and political system. In actual fact, they exhibit a highly literate and artistic adult subversion of the processes of mass loyalty and civil privacy. Their very transgression of the boundaries of public and private language testify to the arbitrariness of the vested interests in the symbiosis between political information and public silence. Behind the antics focused upon by the media lies an articulate expression of the right to participate in the intellectual, linguistic, and artistic resources of the body politic whose members otherwise sicken in silence and obedience. Moreover, these demands come from middle-class, literate students whose very production, in terms of the proliferation of universities and the rationalizations of the educational process, was designed to recruit them to the tasks of the administered economy. These are the men and women who play with gender, dress, work, and authority, who challenge sexism, racism and the exclusion of the welfare poor and homeless. They are also peculiarly the benefactors and the victims of the role of the media in modern politics. As benefactors, they get the coverage and display that fuels the spread of the global protest movement. They are victims insofar as that their bodily antics, clashes, and confrontations serve the media in the conveyance of the palpable disorder and implied irrationality of their demands.

A considerable ideological effort has been made both in the media and academia to erase the body politics of the 1960s from our political memory. Yet, more than ever, people continue to look for reasonable articulations of the body politic in order to express their concern with environmental pollution, genocide, family breakdown, threats to the bodily integrity of women and children, unwholesome food, inadequate medicine, and the like, since these are the issues where political welfare becomes intelligible and valuable to them. Families and individuals want to know what institutions and powers shape their physical and mental health, what determines their conditions of work and their standard of living, as well as what influences the chances of war and peace. From the standpoint of these fundamental concerns, I believe we need to replace the dominant imagery of administrative and organizational science with a four-level model of the body politic.

The *bio-body politic* represents a way of collecting the interest men and women have in their well-being, bodily health, and reproduction. The welfare of the family is iconic of the satisfaction of these demands. The *productive body politic* represents a complex organization of labor and intellect expended in the material and social reproduction of life. Here we speak of an active and creative worker. The *libidinal body politic* represents a level of

Table 3.1 *Body Politic*

Levels	Institutions	Discourse
bio-body	family	well-being, health, sickness
productive body	work	self-control, exploitation
libidinal body	personality	happiness, creativity-discontent
civic body	commons	public, non-positional goods

desire that fulfills the order of personality insofar as it transcends the goods of family and economy and aspires to that highest intelligence, love and happiness. The *civic body politic* represents a common legacy that enables each one in the name of others.

So long as we continue to be birthed and familied of one another, the bodily social, and libidinal orders of living will not be separable worlds although we consider possible re-alignments here in later chapters. By the same token, the body politic cannot be reduced to purely economistic satisfactions any more than to the dream of love's body. It is a distinctive feature of the metaphor of the body politic that it allows us to stand away from *mechano-morphism*, that is, machine, cybernetic, and organization metaphors that (fictionally) reduce the problem of political legitimacy to sheerly cognitivist practices. This shift in turn recovers the *embodied rationalities* of everyday living, family survival, health, self-respect, love, and communion. People – when asked – are aware of the necessary inter-relationships among their family, economic, and personal commitments. They judge the benefits of their labors in the productive sector of the body politic in terms of its returns to their familial and personal lives. They are willing to make trade-offs between the demands of family life and the ambitions of their personal and libidinal lives. In short, ordinary people have a fairly complex understanding of their civic lives that is not reducible to the single pattern of utilitarian or decisionistic reasoning that governs calculations in the economic sector (O'Neill, 1995).

By differentiating the four levels of the body politic, we further separate ourselves from naturalistic accounts of the problem of political legitimacy by introducing a line of ethical development as the fundamental myth of political life. The several levels of family economic, personal and civic life represent a historical-ethical development of anthropomorphosis and also permit us to identify contradictions or constraints and regressions in the body politic. Thus, we can identify alienation as a complex phenomenon that affects not only the productive body but also the bio- and libidinal bodies. Conversely, alienation is not solved merely by satisfying organic needs or by the smooth engineering of productive relations, since these do not meet the demands of the libidinal body. By the same token, we cannot abstract the dreams of libidinal life from our civic commitments to familial and economic life. A critical theory of the legitimacy problem in the body politic is a constitutive theory of civic development and popular recognition of the places where this development is blocked or deteriorating.

The paradox of modern corporate culture is that it panders to the libidinal body, titillating and ravishing its sensibilities, while at the same time it standardizes and packages libidinal responses to its products (O'Neill, 2002b). In North America the libidinal body politic is the creature of the corporate culture and its celebration of the young, white, handsome, heterosexual world of health and affluence. In this sense, it reflects an unhealthy distortion of the community's political life and a denial of the community's failure to cope with the poor, the sick, the aged and those whom it regards as 'colored' people. Everything that fails to conform to the image of suburbinanity has to be segregated and pushed into the ghettos of race, poverty crime, and insanity. It is therefore natural that political struggles over integration in the affluent-racist context of corporate capism take on the imagery of white rape, black power, women's liberation and youth protests. A critical theory of political legitimacy, on the other hand, does not discount the rationality of people's ordinary accounts of their political experience in terms of the vocabularies of family, work, and person. It is for this reason that each of the levels of the body politic is represented in a characteristic institution – the family, the economy, the person and the commons – each is in turn allocated its proper domain of discourse. Although the various institutional and discourse realms of the body politic are analytically differentiated, together they may be said to constitute an evolutionary process in which the congruency of its discursive orders maximizes the common welfare. Every society needs to reproduce itself biologically, materially and spiritually. These needs are articulated at the institutional levels of the family, work, personality and community where discourse focuses upon relevant notions of well-being, health, suffering, estrangement, and self-expression.

Here I cannot deal with the variety of social science knowledge and alternative socioeconomic institutions that are generated at these various levels of the body politic (we shall examine the functions of biomedical discourse in this regard in Chapter 5). I would point out, however, that the articulation of the libidinal body generates discourse demands that impinge differently upon the institutions of family and work, and that, to date, the institutionalization of these 'revolutionary' demands continues to represent a challenge to all modes of scientistic, social, and political knowledge. But even now we can envisage an extension of Habermas's (1984) program for the rational justification of an ideal speech community in terms of the specific discursive pragmatics of the body politic. For such an extension it would be necessary to generate a typology of knowledge and evaluation claims with regard to the bio-body, the productive body and the libidinal body at each appropriate institutional level, with further civic criteria for urgency, democratic force, and the like. The business of politics ought, in some way short of authoritarianism, to foster citizens capable of the good life. Therefore, political legitimacy must be grounded in familied contexts and communities of everyday belief and action that regenerate civic education without subordinating people to a political science outside the life of the body politic:

> To attain and affirm an ideal of family life as the locus of humanization is, contrary to certain unreflective radical orthodoxies, to put pressure upon social structures and arrangements, not to affirm them. For to the extent that the public world, with all its political, economic, bureaucratic force, invades and erodes the private sphere, it, not the private world, should be the target of the social rebel and the feminist critic. To promote a politics of displacement that further erodes the terms of the private sphere and all that stands between us and a course of power or market-ridden definition of all of life, is to repress discourse on public, political issues even as one simultaneously takes the symptoms of its destructive effects as 'good news' that radical change is just around the corner. (Elshtain, 1981: 333)

To start on a positive program, let us insist upon anthropomorphism and civic familism as the root values of political discourse seeking to correct the twin excesses of neo-individualism and minimal governance. To supply civic meaning and value to the identities, decisions, and interpretations generated in the social system as a quasi-natural environment of public life, the following propositions may be asserted in defense of a familied politics:

1   Human beings become human in families.
2   The human family is the first cradle of intelligence, common sense, love, and justice.
3   The human family is the foundation of all civil and political life.
4   Civic familism does not invite retribalism; rather, it repoliticizes the split between our public and private lives.
5   Each family owes to every other family the right to posterity.
6   Every family is a witness to the integrity or holiness of the human society.

As Elshtain insists, it can never be too late to rebuild the civic family in the interest of fortifying our public life. Indeed, every premature pronouncement of the family's end can only strengthen the state at the expense of those very individuals who place their hope in the socioeconomic processes that lead to defamilization (O'Neill, 1982c). Since the 1970s we have been caught up in a curious mixture of commercialism and mean welfarism that has sold us the ideal of nuclear family in a form suburbanized and standardized to the point of inanity. It is this family haven which has collapsed, thrown itself into the arms of the law, psychoanalysis, and medicine. It has nonetheless been used as a model for working-class and marginalized families, though their ways of holding together and coming apart are different. In short, we cannot overlook that the family has been stripped of many of its civic functions and reduced to a phase in the lives of individuals whose primary goals are found in school, work, and consumption (Busaca and Ryan, 1982; Hacker, 1982). Indeed, many individuals who turned away from the absurd privatization of the 1950s' family did so to restore intimacy and personality in the political realm during the revolutionary 1960s.

We are experiencing a massive shift in our conception of where and how people are to be produced. A few decades ago such a statement would have raised the horrible vision of an animal farm, a state-medical hatchery in which familied life was a lost memory, a dream punishable by the state guardians. Today we cannot imagine the family outside of the therapeutic state (Lasch, 1980). At the same time, our commercial imagination exploits the family as a haven, madhouse, and a gadget station used by loosely connected relatives, as we shall see in the following chapters. Because capism desires, in terms of its own technological myth, to replace human beings with machines, it is driven, however faultily, to try to replace familied society and labor with a consumerized society. The latter is underwritten by its industrial, legal, and medical technology and a variety of neo-individualist ideologies that seek to reshape our notions of men, women, and children, from familied beings into beings whose rights and duties are defined through the neo-liberal state. In such a state the political animal is more of an animal than a political creature since neo-liberalism increases privacy at the expense of public life. What I have in mind here refers to more than the historical accumulation of goods and services. It involves a sociolegal redefinition of the family for the consumption tasks of late capism. A major pedagogic and therapeutic switch is involved in which family attitudes are 'engineered' on behalf of the industrial, commercial, and state system of late capism. The working family is increasingly subjected to degradation in favor of the family wise in consumption. This involves the degradation of household work, cooking, cleaning, caring in any way that does not bring the family into the orbit of industry commerce, and professionalism. Simultaneously, the family that is wired into such commercialism and professionalism in the delivery of its functions is elevated. The result, of course, is that the family again splits.

The bourgeois family, whose professional members service themselves in saving the working-class family, becomes the principal circuit of defamilized and feminized discourse upon family health, education, and welfare. Thus children's health, education and consumer awareness are the discursive channels for the reorientation of the families to the new demands of late capism. Bourgeois feminism and the legal, medical, and educational professions, as well as commercial advertising, all combine to subordinate the family 'patriarch' to his more enlightened women and children:

> In the death of patriarchy, both libertarians and business shared an interest. Yet their interests were at odds with one another … The commodified answers to the questions of 'how to live' began to take on a distinctive character. Utilizing the collective image of the family, the ads in their contribution to mass culture did their best to deny that collectively. Each aspect of the family *collective* – the source of decision making, the locus of child rearing, the things which elicited

> affectionate response – all of these now pointed outward toward the world of commodities for their direction. Corporate America had begun to define itself as *the father of us all*. (Ewen, 1976: 184)

It is easy to recall endless advertisements, comic strips, cartoons, kids' movies, and family movies that dramatize the end of the patriarchal family and its surrender to *consumer matriarchy* sponsored by pseudopaternalist corporations. These scenarios have made Hollywood America the symbol of freedom for millions of people whose families, marriages, and communities kept their noses to the grindstone of authority and scarcity. The besieged family and its wayward antics are the staple of American lawlessness, smiled upon by American law itself, so often the clown in the comedy (O'Neill, 2002b). In reality the American family is as much exploited in these scenes as are the still grim industrial and monotonous suburban settings that furnish their background. The tragicomedy, however, is played out differently in the towns and in the country, or in the middle-, upper- and working-class, immigrant families. This results in huge problems of public health and morality, of criminality and ignorance which beset the ideology of individual self-development. At the same time the neo-liberal state reinforces neo-individualism while simultaneously professionalizing and bureaucratizing the sociolegal practices that correct its failures (Bledstein, 1978).

There remains the analytic task of seeing how divergent discursive strategies developed around the family as a bulwark against the state and simultaneously as the factor that limits criticism and revolt directed against the social order. The liberal bourgeois conception of state and economic relations meant that the bourgeoisie had to find a solution to the problem of pauperism without generating socialism even though granting rights to work, education, and welfare. Simultaneously the bourgeoisie had to find a new basis for social commitment on the part of the masses while excluding them from political participation. As Jacques Donzelot shows, two strategies of control came to be preferred: (a) philanthropy; and (b) medicine-hygiene. The two strategies were designed to transform the family into a buffer against pauperism, on the one hand, by shoring up the practice of family savings and family assistance, and against irresponsible patriarchy on the other, by defending standards of health and morality due to children. Thus, from both sides the family became the focus of philanthropic and therapeutic strategies designed to raise its reproductive potential with respect to the economy and the social order without absolute state interference. By the same token, the family was saved by having its autonomy reduced *vis-à-vis* the therapeutic state, which served the liberal bourgeois concept of society without socialism. It is no accident, then, that in certain respects the laws on divorce go hand in hand with state laws that undermine patriarchal and familial authority over children: the liberalization of the heterosexual marriage contract is a trade-off for the state's becoming the parent of last resort:

> The modern family is not so much an institution as a *mechanism*. It is through the disparity of the familial configurations (the working class and bourgeois bipolarity), the variances between individual interests and the family interest, that this mechanism operates. Its strength lies in a social *architectonics* whose characteristic feature is always to couple an exterior intervention with conflicts or differences of potential within the family: the protection of poor children which allowed for the destruction of the family as an island of resistance; the privileged alliance of the doctor and the educator with the wife for developing procedures of savings, educational promotion and so on. The procedures of social control depend much more on the complexity of intrafamilial relationships than on its complexes, more on its craving for betterment than on the defense of its acquisitions (private property, judicial rigidity). A wonderful mechanism, since it enables the social body to deal with marginality through a near-total dispossession of private rights, and to encourage positive integration, the renunciation of the question of political right through the private pursuit of wellbeing. (Donzelot, 1979: 94)

We have always to remember that the tendencies I am describing are never in practice wholly congruent with one another. Thus it is possible to see much family law as having delivered married women from the arbitrary authority of their husbands, restoring child custody to them and releasing them from sexual abuse and violence. These changes have considerably altered the intrafamilial status of wives. But while the state holds out on day care services and women continue to be weak wage earners, their rights in family law do not match the structural realities of the working women's economy. It is a difficult matter to decide upon the extent to which the state oppresses women rather than men. Indeed, the question has no general answer in this form (Brophy and Smart, 1981; McIntosh, 1978). It can be approached only relative to specific historical stages and policies of capitalism and the liberal state. The ideological function of welfare, social work, and social policy as state apparatuses has been noted by Elizabeth Wilson:

> Social policy is simply one aspect of the capitalism state, an acceptable face of capitalism, and social welfare policies amount to no less than the *State organization of domestic life*. Women encounter state repression within the very bosom of the family. This may seem paradoxical when the ideology of individualism and private property that has grown with capitalism has stressed the sanctity of family privacy But in many ways the Welfare State, like the position of women, is full of paradox and contradiction. (Wilson, 1977: 9)

Juliet Mitchell has argued that we need to distinguish a number of factors at work in the history of women's inferior social position, rather than contend simply that their biological status diminishes their value at work while increasing it in reproductive relations. In order to provide a stage-specific historical analysis of the structure of exploitative relations ruling women, she proposed (in the mid-1960s) to speak of four structures determining women's social value: (1) production; (2) reproduction; (3) sex; and (4) the socialization of children. Women's emancipation cannot be treated as a sort of idealization of socialist freedom. It requires specific and continuous legislation in the field of equal work conditions and remuneration, contraceptive practices, the mutuality of sexual experience, and new agencies for child socialization:

> In practical terms this means a coherent system of demands. The four elements of women's condition cannot merely be considered each in isolation; they form a structure of specific inter-relations. The contemporary bourgeois family can be seen as a triptych of sexual, reproductive, and socializatory functions (the women's world) embraced by production (the men's world) – precisely a structure which in the final instance is determined by the economy. The exclusion of women from production – social human activity – and their confinement to a monolithic condensation of functions in a unity – the family – which is precisely unified in the *natural* part of each function, is the root cause of the contemporary *social* definition of women as *natural* beings. Hence the main thrust of any emancipation movement must still concentrate on the economic element – the entry of women fully into public industry. (Mitchell, 1966)

Whatever the difficulties, the civic status of women continues to be an issue in modern society. We can expect continuing reforms along several lines – reforms whose achievement would be difficult to imagine without the struggle in which women are engaged in pursuit of something like the following basic civil rights for all women:

1   the right to equal opportunity;
2   the right to equal employment opportunity;
3   the right to sexual equality;
4   the right to control conception;
5   the right to bodily integrity in the widest sense to cover rape, pornography, abuse, and medical exploitation.

In calling attention to the phenomenon of bio-politics, I do not mean to adopt a totally negative view of the modern therapeutic state. This is because I am a child of the UK welfare state, the rich recipient of its employment, health, housing and educational supplements to working-class families whose market fates are otherwise perilous (O'Neill, 1995). It is one thing to be critical of the bureaucratic snags in the welfare state. It is quite another to exchange the civic aspiration of a welfare society for the lean and exclusionary practice of the US social security system (Esping-Andersen, 1990). Nor should we allow insane versions of eugenics to deter us from modeling the general health, education and well-being of families and individuals otherwise rationed out by market forces. Indeed, it is the market that commits us to the rhetoric of Darwinian fitness and to market-designed reproduction, health, fitness and intelligence. The twentieth-century horrors of state-driven eugenics/genocide should keep us on the alert. The present wave of neo-liberal anti-governance has perhaps reduced such misadventures (give or take the containment of total nuclear death). What remains to be seen is how the market will redefine well-being in terms of *individual bio-medical risk* for which smart pre-emptive interventions will be devised. Between this promise and the reality of delivery lie huge moral and political questions regarding ownership/access to genetic codes, since the technologies involved are extraordinarily costly. At the same time, we are now intent on claiming a fundamental *biological citizenship* (Rose, 2001). Between the genetic and the political promise, the quality of human life remains hugely dependent upon the practical value of good-enough civic institutions.

4

Consumer Bodies

In this chapter I want to return to the most familiar image of the body – the body that has *needs*. Between birth and death, we do many things simply to maintain the body as the instrument of much else we seek. For the moment neglecting those intrauterine needs that are present even from the time of conception and leaving aside those that are present even in the process of dying, we may think of life in between these points as the ceaseless pursuit of satisfactions pressed upon us by our bodily condition. We need food, drink, clean air, rest, shelter, clothing, a certain standard of public health and safety; and we need these things both to sustain life and to reproduce it in a reasonably healthy population whose offspring will have a fair chance of survival.

Bodily needs might then be considered *basic* needs – their satisfaction constituting the simple but sound pleasures of living that Plato described for the 'first city':

> Let us begin, then, with a picture of our citizens' manner of life, with the provisions we have made for them. They will be producing corn and wine, and making clothes and shoes. When they have built their houses, they will mostly work without their coats or shoes in the summer, and in winter be well shoed and clothed. For their food, they will prepare flour and barley-meal for kneading and baking, and set out a grand spread of loaves and cakes on rushes or fresh leaves. Then they will lie on beds of myrtle-boughs and byrony and make merry with their children, drinking their wine after the feast with garlands on their heads and singing the praises of the gods. So they will live pleasantly together; and a prudent fear of poverty or war will keep them from begetting children beyond their means. (*The Republic*, BK II, 372A)

Ours, however, is an ambivalent legacy. In the Judeo-Christian tradition, our bodies are a fallen version of those that Adam and Eve once enjoyed. Having succumbed to Eve's curiosity our bodies now suffer a life of hard labor, ending in death:

> To the woman he said
> 'I will greatly multiply your pain in childbearing;
> in pain you shall bring forth children,
> yet your desire shall be for your husband,
> And he shall rule over you.'
> and to Adam he said,
> 'Because you have listened to the voice of your wife,
> and have eaten of the tree of which I commanded you, "You shall not eat of it",
> cursed is the ground because of you: in toil you shall eat of it
> all the days of your life;

thorns and thistles it shall bring forth to you;
and you shall eat the plants of the field.
In the sweat of your face you shall eat bread
till you return to the ground, for out of it you were taken;
you are dust, and to dust you shall return.'
(Gen. 3:16–19)

We are chained, then, to the alternating pleasures and pains of the body's satisfaction. Now it is clear that in terms of that other biblical injunction, that man should be lord of the earth, we have created a great civilization within which the necessities of life and the conditions of labor and consumption have been refined almost beyond imagination. Intellectual, artistic, scientific, culinary, medical, legal, political, and even military culture expands beyond any level that can be contained by the simple standard of bodily need. Indeed, the proliferation of civilizational or cultural needs has been so overwhelming that it has always provoked religious, moral, and social thinkers to try to find a base line between natural or primary needs and secondary or excessive and *unnatural* needs. Such efforts to discriminate between primary and secondary needs have been motivated by the problem of good and evil, by the problem of poverty in the midst of plenty, and by a nostalgia for modes of living that seem less egoistic, less competitive and inauthentic than life in societies ruled by the constant drive to accumulate wealth, power, and privilege.

Turning the pages of any modern magazine or scanning TV is enough to cause us to discover that we are still consumed with the problem of *authentic* human needs but quite unable to erase the line between lives that celebrate unlimited affluence and a world of misery where millions still lack rudimentary food and shelter. In either case, the body is the icon of abundance and misery, of dieting and starvation, of sexuality and mutilation. This paradox has provoked a number of attempts to discover a fundamental economic anthropology. In particular, it requires us to rethink the relation between material and symbolic culture already considered (in Chapter 2) and I propose now to develop some arguments in this direction, while preserving my chosen focus upon the political economy of the body. The dilemma from which we start is the nature of our own economy. In offering to meet our every need, it seems less to serve us than to enslave us. As Galbraith observes, it is as though our economy were ruled by an evil genius:

> Were it so that a man on arising each morning was assailed by demons which instilled in him a passion sometimes for silk shirts, sometimes for kitchenware, sometimes for chamber pots, sometimes for orange squash, there would be every reason to applaud the effort to find the goods, however odd, that quenched this flame. But should it be that his passion was the result of his first having cultivated the demons, and should it also be that his effort to allay it stirred the demons to even greater and greater effort, there would be question as to how rational was his solution. Unless restrained by conventional attitudes, he might wonder if the solution lay with more goods or fewer demons.

> So it is that if production creates the wants it seeks to satisfy, or if the wants emerge *pari passu* with the production, then the urgency of the wants can no longer be used to defend the urgency of the production. Production only fills a void that it has itself created. (Galbraith, 1958: 153)

To the ancients, the excess of modern experience would have been no surprise. Indeed, Galbraith's imagery of the demonic forces of unleashed consumption captures the idiocy of any society engaged in the pursuit of order based upon passion. In Plato's *Republic,* for example, it is this tendency that is subdued by making the passions subject to a hierarchy of moral and intellectual pursuits whose fixed relative place guarantees the healthy order of society. In such a system, it would be monstrous to think of the passions, or of the merchant and laboring elements, ruling those who think and defend the social order. Even on the eve of modern society it appeared convincing to Hobbes that the passion for power could be brought to order only in an authoritarian state that canceled man's pride and fear (Oakeshott, 1967; Hirschman, 1977). In contrast, the remarkable assertion is made in Adam Smith's *The Wealth of Nations* (1817) that if men would only restrict themselves to trading in their *private passions*, there would result a *public order* more secure than anything church or state could guarantee. Moreover, it was held that church and state would reveal a higher morality by leaving the market free. For if ever morality were to prevail over vice, the economy would collapse and church and state with it:

> For the main design of the Fable, (as it is breefly explain'd in the Moral) is to shew the Impossibility of enjoying all the most elegant Comforts of Life that are to be met within an industrious, wealthy and powerful Nation, and at the same time be bless'd with all the Virtue and Innocence that can be wish'd for in a Golden Age; from thence to expose the Unreasonableness and Folly of those, that desirous of being an opulent and flourishing People, and wonderfully greedy after all the Benefits they can receive as such, are yet always murmuring at and exclaiming against those Vices and Inconveniencies, that from the beginning of the World to this present Day, have been inseparable from all Kingdoms and States that ever were fam'd for Strength, Riches and Politeness at the same time. (Mandeville, 1970: 54–5)

To those of us still puzzled by the variety of good and evil and the inextricable mixture of sense and nonsense in our lives, Mandeville's *The Fable of the Bees* remains a consolation. Yet the fact is that it is precisely in those societies where the economy is highly autonomous that the crown is still disputed between consumption and production.

Critics like Galbraith believe that consumption can be made more rational only if we devise a rational agenda for production. Despite the theorists of consumer sovereignty and with just a little attention to advertising, it is obvious that consumer needs are generated in the productive sector rather than in the consumer's body, however his or her demons may push. But this dependence effect as such is not responsible for the irrationality of consumer behavior. For, as we shall see, economic anthropology reveals that in every society wants are largely cultural acquisitions. In the case of our own society therefore, we cannot understand the arrangement of the economic agenda in favor of private consumption over public consumption (except where the latter, for this very reason, is stigmatized as poor relief or welfare benefits even when declared a citizen's right) unless we adopt a *semiological* approach to commodity functions. To repeat an earlier shibboleth, we must try to see what it is that *commodities are good for thinking* as well as what it is they are good for consuming. Taking the latter route gets us into all the difficulties of trying to think apart necessary and unnecessary goods despite the fact that each is in someone's interest to produce and consume. We find ourselves looking for religious, moral, and historical benchmarks that might point to the primacy of necessary and natural consumption as the guide to an economy that would remain subordinate to the overall social order.

In *The Theory of the Leisure Class* (1925), Veblen argued that what confers upon the pursuit of wealth its insatiable nature is not its function of satisfying natural needs so much as its accommodation to the pursuit of an insatiable need for *social prestige*. Social man does not live by bread alone. Socialists have nevertheless managed to read Veblen's message as though it restricted conspicuous consumption to bourgeois man. They have imagined that in so-called primitive societies and in future communist societies the prestige economy would be absent. The other side of the coin is that capitalists are not free to universalize 'status seeking' because we find it functioning in potlatch societies on the Pacific Northwest coast of Canada, in the United States, and even in the Soviet Union. Rather, what the anthropological evidence seems to reveal is that preindustrial societies regulate exchanges in a two-tier system: (1) the *subsistence* economy; and (2) the *prestige* or ceremonial economy. Even among the famous Kwakiutl, subsistence goods played no part in the prestige economy which was restricted to the accumulation of blankets and large pieces of engraved copper. Where there was an exchange between the two systems, it was regulated, as Mary Douglas (Douglas and Isherwood, 1979) shows, so that people did not amass subsistence goods at the expense of their neighbors. In fact, it is possible to argue that the prestige economy had, through feasts, a redistributive function, correcting imbalances in the subsistence economy.

In our own economy we seem unable to distinguish between subsistence and prestige economics (Harris, 1978; Leiss, 1978; Packard, 1959). Although we speak of guaranteed minimum-wage levels, the goods upon which this money is spent are not kept separate from the prestige economy which redefines simple use-values in invidious terms of consumption, style, and class position. So-called transfer payments and most public-sector goods like health and education facilities are regarded as adjustments to their counterparts in the private sector. Consider the trouble we experienced until very recently in redesigning the automobile. If the automobile were merely a means of transportation, the task of recreating smaller, more fuel-efficient cars – not to mention shifting the transportation of people to buses and trains – would be simple. But the automobile is a symbolic good. It is the vehicle not only of bodies but of bodies who value the ideas of privacy and freedom. The automobile is therefore as much a vehicle of individual ideology as of anything else it might carry. To accommodate this automotive ideology we have subordinated vast amounts of space to roadways and parking areas; we have suburbanized our cities and turned country villages into shopping centers; and we have vastly altered the quality of everyday life with noise, pollution, and loss of life and limb in favor of a machine that promises us youth, beauty and sexual and social mobility.

> The car is a status symbol, it stands for comfort, power, authority and speed, *it is consumed as a sign* in addition to its practical use, its various significances involving, intensifying and neutralizing each other as it stands for consumption and consumer symbols, symbolizes happiness and procures happiness by symbols. (Lefebvre, 1971: 102–3)

As a *symbolic vehicle*, therefore, the automobile circulates between the economy of use (transportation) and the economy of prestige (power, energy, style). As such, it is perfectly geared to express the cultural value we place upon technology, private property, individual mobility, sexual rivalry, and social competition. Despite its claims, it is not only the Volvo that is the thinking man's car. In our society all cars are good to think as well as drive.

We began by trying on the notion that the meeting of simple subsistence needs might give primacy to consumption and thereby make production to meet those needs rational or reasonable. But we have found that as social bodies we are committed to much more than our own biological and material reproduction. As communicative bodies we are involved in the consumption and (re)production of the culture and society we inhabit. We cannot, therefore, treat the economy as a production process set in motion by consumption and determined solely by its material logic. We have to rethink the language of consumption and production. Above all, we have to learn to set aside the logocentric notion of the sovereign consumer assembling utilities according to his/her own rational schedules of need. This is precisely how the *ideological* conception of consumption functions as a myth of bourgeois thought. We cannot say what an American car is without knowing what it is that American society thinks and does with cars. People other than Americans also have their mythologies of the automobile. Consider, for example, Roland Barthes' comment on the Citroën D.S. (there is a play on words involved; D.S. as pronounced in French sounds the same as *déesse*, goddess):

> It is obvious that the new Citroën has fallen from the sky inasmuch as it appears at first sight as a superlative *object*. We must not forget that an object is the best messenger of a world above nature: one can easily see in an object at once a perfection and an absence of origin, a closure and a brilliance, a transformation of life onto matter (matter is much more magical than life), and in a word a *silence* which belongs to the realm of fairy tales. The D.S. – the 'Goddess' – has all the features (or at least the public is unanimous in attributing them to it at first sight) of one of those objects from another universe which

have supplied fuel for the neomania of the eighteenth century and that of our own science-fiction: the *Déesse* is *first and foremost* a new *Nautilus*. (Barthes, 1973: 88)

As an object, therefore, the automobile functions as a token in a larger discourse. The same is true of needs. We cannot restrict needs to the biobody. Indeed, as we shall see, even bioneeds are symbolically mediated to function in the larger discourse of the medicalized society and its therapeutic ideology.

I am not recommending the study of 'distorting' sociopsychological and sociosomatic effects upon otherwise rational economic behavior. Rather, I am proposing to rethink the categories of consumption, production, and distribution in terms of the semiotics or *rhetoric of commodities* as discourse types signifying a variety of social domains ranging from subsistence to fantasy:

> The logic of exchange is therefore primordial. In some ways, the individual is nothing (any more than the object we were talking about at first), and a given language (of words, women, or commodities) is what exists first, as a social form in respect of which there are no individuals since it is a structure of exchange. This structure arises from a logic of differentiation working simultaneously on two levels:
>
> 1 It differentiates the human elements of exchange into pairs that are not individuated but distinct and tied by the rule of exchange.
> 2 It differentiates the material elements of exchange into distinct, therefore meaningful, elements.
>
> Language exists, first of all – not as an absolute, autonomous *system* but as a structure of exchange contemporaneous with meaning itself and within which the individual articulates what he wants to say. In the same fashion, 'consumption' does not exist because of an objective need to consume, or some final intention in the subject vis-à-vis the object. Through a system of exchange there develops the social production of differentiated materials and of a code of meanings and established values. The functionality of goods and individual needs supervenes, adjusting itself to, rationalizing, and repressing these fundamental structural mechanisms. (Baudrillard, 1972: 76–7)

Let us glance at Plato's *Republic* once again. In the construction of his perfect state, Plato distinguishes between a first and a second city. He begins by imagining a first city in which people eat and drink simply and do little more than is required to sustain and reproduce their families: For some reason this situation is unstable, and the people begin to expand their wants. In the second city there is no simple way of relating decisions to the features of the natural setting. Desires are complex, commodities abound, and good and evil cease to be distinguishable without the specific work of philosophy and politics, which henceforth must rule the body and subjugate the economy that characterizes the modern world. Yet the economy remains a very moral order. It claims to be in the service of worldwide human need, and it is the setting for displays of creativity, intelligence, and foresight that it in turn rewards as evidence of its own good auspices. The modern economy makes a powerful claim to be the sole source of the good life and the principal training ground of the moral qualities required for its successful production, if not consumption. Looked at in this way, the stratification system, so far from being an evil, acts as a moral screen, a device for representing the stages in the good life rather than any obstacle to its pursuit.

Marx argued that all production is social. I want to include in the notion of production not just the expenditure of physical labor but also the employment of *every technique of the body in a unified field of production and consumption*. By this I mean that we must regard the *productive body* as an extension of the economy and not simply as a factor of production like labor. Like its labor power, the fetishizations of the productive body exist only in a market economy capable of reifying its stress, relaxation, health, illness, beauty, spontaneity, and sexuality. The reification of the body into productive sectors concerned with its own production and consumption integrates and redistributes the body throughout the social division of labor. Thus the productive body is not a factor of production in the way that Marx thought of land, labor, and capital. The productive body is integrated into the division of labor both internally – for example, through modern medicine – and externally – for example, through fashion and cosmetics. Thus the productive body is both an extension and an intensification of the space, time and activity of the modern economy. To be sure, the economy expropriates the labor of the body subjecting it to pain in its tasks and to an unsatisfactory standard of living in return for its wages. But consumers can also be taught to devalue their biological bodies entirely except as those bodies are reappraised in the willing consumption of industrially mediated experience, looks, attitudes, and characters. The modern economy aspires to control the socially significant points of entry and exit in the life cycle, prematurely declaring young persons worldly-wise and old persons obsolescent. Every physical, mental, and emotional need of persons may be reified as a chemical agent or professional service. Thus, unless we learn to resist and to refuse, what was once self-knowledge and personal identity will amount to nothing other than the consumerized capacity to refer a residual self to fashion.

The most massive exploitation of the body occurs whenever the economy teaches us to devalue our body unless it has been sold grace, spontaneity, vivaciousness, bounce, confidence, smoothness, and freshness. Here the economy is a principal socializing agency in those techniques of the body that display the cultural values of youth, aggression, mobility, and sociability. By the same token, it is obliged to hide the ordinary condition of men, women, and children. As life becomes more sedentary and less physically demanding (though a certain myth is at work here – notice how many people are tired!), the economy is able to sell physical activity as recreation, fitness, and sport. The vicarious consumption of bodily experiences is a further characteristic of mass society. It extends from sport to the theater, and thereby makes violence and sexuality principal ingredients of these commodities. The more modern families are geared to consumption, the more they divide into wage earners who separate sexuality and reproduction. Thus the female body must be romanticized and deployed as the instrument of rational and contractual associations. Trusting to the pill – condom usage remains random – young women's bodies are made mobile for work, high-rise living, and adventure.

The modern economy, then, engages us in an enormous expansion of wants and desires while claiming to satisfy these desires in ethical ways (Sahlins, 1976: 166–204). The two sides of this equation are production and consumption. From economics we receive only a general notion of the human labor that goes into work and consumption. We know that much work even today requires bodily labor, physical and nervous pain. We know less about consumption, as is evident from the largely metabolic metaphor we use to describe our relations to commodities, many of which have little to do with eating or drinking and whose use can hardly be understood by means of any such analogy. I believe we need to think of the *work of consumption* in order to begin to understand what is required of us in the collection, display, and disposal of commodities that service the collective representation of a scientific and technical culture. It is essential that the consumer is not born but is produced by *anxiety-inducing* processes that teach him and her to want to want things that service needs which arose in the first place only from commercial invention. As a result, consumers must learn *economic sacrifice*, that is to say everyone must learn that it is imperative to keep up with the economy's futuristic production of needs and satisfactions by putting aside present needs of the self in favor of the future self or its family.

> The result of this, we believe, is that the activities which keep people moving in a class society which make them seek more money, more possessions, higher-status jobs, do not originate in a materialistic desire, or even sensuous appreciation of things, but out of an attempt to restore a psychological deprivation that class structure has effected in their lives. In other words, *the psychological motivation instilled by a class society is to heal a doubt about the self rather than create more power over things and other persons in the world.* (Sennett and Cobb, 1973: 171)

The economics of consumption is only partially illuminated by the bodily metaphor with which it is glossed – though perhaps the light is equal to that shed on the supply side by the bodily metaphor of production. Economists conceal that production is painful or thoughtful, yet consider consumption easy, pleasant, and costless. Ideally, i.e., to avoid alternative psychologies, economists prefer to operate with a disembodied subject, an abstract pain/pleasure calculator whose own operation costs nothing. Even though the stock market shamelessly displays moods of elation and depression, *there are no perplexed, harassed, tired, disappointed, crazy consumers in economics.* Above all, there are no housewives, husbands, children, old folk, or families for whom consumer sovereignty is an irony, given the way they have to make household decisions in the market and work place. In short, economists have largely ignored the *work of consumption*. The bewildering range of consumer choices, of brands, weights, and ingredients, not to mention the choices in styles, locations, and scenarios of living, relaxing, entertaining, and the like is apt to call for considerable effort from the consumer – so much, in fact, that without the help of servants, he or she may be overwhelmed by the burdens of consumption – as two income families now find, reinventing delivery services. Hence the further imposition placed upon us by self-service establishments, which exact considerable labor from us.

We do not literally consume automobiles, television sets, furniture, houses, clothing, cosmetics, and entertainment. Does this mean, then, that they do not involve our bodies? Rather, we must ask, how do they involve our bodies? We need to clothe, house, and transport our bodies, just as we need to feed them. But there are now very particular relationships between these necessities. Thus, as urban centers lie at greater distances from the centers of food production, food is increasingly processed and packaged for its life in transport and supermarkets. This secondary necessity involves the use of chemical ingredients in the food chain (as well as genetically modified crops) which may reduce its nutritional value, and even make it harmful. To eat such food might now be considered *work*, risking an industrial injury such as cancer on behalf of the urban/industrial complex. In the middle class, where consumption is a heavy obligation – and where (until global labor eased the problem) servants are hardly obtainable – we find an elaborate 'role-set' in which the husband/wife team serves as janitor, gardener, cook, chauffeur, host, parent, lover, and friend in a single day. Galbraith (1973) is virtually alone among economists in noticing the reality of the household economy and in particular the tasks of women, hitherto ignored by classical economics. Economists presume upon the *cryptoservant* role of women in the administration of the household consumption process. They may or may not have noticed its celebration in advertising. But in their calculations of GNP, they hide the female production of household goods and services:

> In few other matters has the economic system been so successful in establishing values and molding resulting behavior to its needs as in the shaping of womanly attitude and behavior. And ... the economic importance of the resulting achievement is great. Without women to administer it, the possibility of increasing consumption would be sharply circumscribed. With women assuming the tasks of administration, consumption can be more or less indefinitely increased. In very high income households this administration becomes ... an onerous task. But even here expansion is still possible; at these levels women tend to be better educated and better administrators. And the greater availability of divorce allows of a measure of trial and error to obtain the best. Thus it is women in their cryptoservant role who make an indefinitely increasing consumption possible. As matters now stand, (and for as long as they so stand), it is their supreme contribution to the modern economy. (Galbraith, 1973: 39–40)

Having observed so much, Galbraith nevertheless fails to see that it is one thing to expose the economic ideology of the consumer woman and quite another to treat the modern family as though it were nothing but a consumption factory in which the formerly productive males have lost any need for a consuming female counterpart. Having observed the reduction of the male productive function, Galbraith (1973: 39–40) goes right on to argue for female independence as something that can be acquired only through control over a wage earned in the market place. Surely the larger economic and political phenomenon is *the consumerization of males and females alike* (and, of course, children), with productive economic decisions removed to the higher levels of the economy. This split is not altered by admitting women into either level of the economy, at least for as long as we retain some line between the consumption imperative and earning a wage. Whether or not he sees this problem, Galbraith in effect moves his argument for the emancipation of women to the thesis that as the economy shifts from the secondary to tertiary stages, i.e., to the predominance of services over things, the female administration of consumption will decline, services being self-consuming and requiring little administration. But since services tend to be either labor-intensive or intellect-intensive, it is difficult to see how they assure emancipation for anyone employed in them – witness the ironies of self-service!

The consumer produces himself and herself provided he, she and children can be sufficiently defamilized, decommunalized, and rendered déclassé. Everything that weakens families fosters the illusion of individual self-production and strengthens consumerism. If there is any central covenant in such a family, it centers upon a mutual regard for the television wherein such arrangements are commercially celebrated (O'Neill, 2002a). What is seen is the war of each against all; mothers and fathers stupified by their children; husbands and wives stupified by one another – above all, everyone stupified by their common admiration for commodities. What is more, as the family self-faulted in its capacity to rearrange itself for con-sumerism, it was aided by the corporate domestication of women's rights and sit-com parodies of paternalism:

> As the rise of capitalism had put traditional family life into disarray, it also joined in on the feminist argument that patriarchal society was antiquated and oppressive ... Yet while feminism had looked toward a world in which women would appropriate control over their own lives, the corporate debunking of the patriarchy coincided with a general devaluation of all forms of self direction. In hailing the *modern woman* as a 'home manager' and in celebrating the child as the conscience of the new age, corporate ideologues asserted that each was expected to devote a high degree of obedience to the directives of the con-sumer market. The industrial elevation of women and children served to relegate the traditional patriarch to an antediluvian, sometimes comic characterization. Here mass culture shared the radical hopes for autonomy and equality. Yet once again, in its depiction of the modern family, the world of mass consumption faltered before the edge of change; as the father of old was relegated to the 'dustbin of history,' the corporate patriarch was crowned as a just and benefi-cent authority for a modern age. (Ewen, 1976: 201–2)

Capital culture is at once elite and mass culture, both productive and con-sumptive, technical and carnal. It provides both the necessities and the excesses of everyday life. Capital culture is at our service. It therefore advertises itself in the first place as the universal provider of necessities formerly beyond the masses. At the same time, however, capital culture recodes excesses as necessities. The result is that elite production is subordinated to consumption as life-style agency and discrimination. In this culture, elites survive by avoiding obsolescence – but for a limited time only – and the mass bears the stigma of second-hand life-style and down-sized desire. We may also think of the restructuring of global and local economies in terms of two shopping agents. The outlets for high fashion commodities service the global, nomadic capital bodies which reproduce themselves through constant shifts in style of dress, food, location, and locomotion. In turn, this world is serviced by less willfully mobile, lesser paid, lesser unionized, more female, coloured and young service workers. But in the process the old order signifiers of class, race and gender become sublimated markers of *class-as-lifestyle*, i.e., individuated performance of options for making something of oneself regarded as a marketable resource in a world where everyone is a 'sales' person. In such a world solidarity is experienced only on the level of performance anxiety since we all have to be 'on' (mobile phones) for someone else, if not the person who serves us. What separates us is

1 the thinness of the actor's resources for staging the service that services us both; not past accumulation but present level of desire;
2 level of absorption of the pedagogy of consumer products as guides in the constant updating of lifestyles;
3 indifference to high/low culture contrasts, including university education and political ideologies that activate class, gender and race as oppositional narratives;
4 pragmatic commitment to university education as site of multi-cultural performances that redistribute traditional and self-referential agency to avoid intergenerational obsolescence in career and personality markets;
5 willingness to recode class division and conflict in terms of in-style/out-of-style performances in the world of work, education and leisure.

We know that the world is a kind of body which suffers, as we do, from misuse. In terms of the *world body politic*, we are faced with striking inequalities in access to food, housing, clothing, health, and life expectancy. A relatively small part of the world monopolizes its resources, suffering from obesity, mental illness, and boredom, while most of humankind, often in the service of the over-privileged industrial countries, slaves to gain a bare existence. Worse still, as new countries enter the path of economic development, their diets tend to change toward the consumption of more meat, sugar, eggs, and foods high in animal-fat content. They simultaneously enter the cycle of coronary heart diseases, diabetes, hypertension, and bowel cancer. Paradoxically, malnutrition is as associated with overeating as with the lack of food. In their constant search for basic raw materials the comfortable nations are also able to displace war and exploitation onto the poorer nations, disrupting their lives even further. The human family has a long way to go before it lives together. A vast number of men, women, and children are still fighting for:

1 the right to satisfy their hunger
2 the right to education
3 the right to work for a living
4 the right to be cared for
5 the right to political organization and freedom of expression.

The terrible thing is that no one's appetite is cut by another's hunger. This is the moral problem facing all industrial societies so long as they continue to generate incredible differences both between their own members and between themselves and other societies whose economies are weaker. If only a small reduction were made in the world's military capacity for self-destruction, a reasonable floor might be set for the living standard of the world's population.

One can hardly escape falling back upon the human body as an image for the development of a balanced social and world order. I do not mean that in order to realize such a state we need to reduce humans to a single pattern of living. Moreover, to attain something like *a world right to life*, we cannot do without complex technical and social aid. Nevertheless, what we must avoid is the temptation to attribute any moral superiority to Western industrial societies over the societies they are currently in a position to help. Industrial and industrializing societies must increasingly confront the question of how they can work in complementary ways with family and local resources. In fact, there is reason to believe that *we need more than ever to reinvent the institution of the family* as a responsible unit of civic action regarding the welfare of its members in matters of education, consumption, and general health. Here, as so often, progress looks like recycling tradition, even while it requires of us an ever greater critical intelligence to avoid fundamentalism.

5

Medical Bodies

In earlier chapters we have seen how the body politic functions on the economic and political level. It is a complex task to analyze the simultaneous celebration and degradation of the human body in the production, consumption, and administrative processes of modern political economy. What we have observed so far reaches its apogee in the *medicalization* of the body. Here we have a new frontier for industrial societies. Here, above all, is a place for the choreography of professional heroism: one body probing another in the extension of the finest technology in the world. No scenario is better suited to modern society. Its apparent classlessness, its obvious expertise, and its secular humanism are not only the very stuff of medical soap operas; they are our elemental ideology. It is beyond the competence of any single scientist to keep abreast of all the developments in medical biology. Indeed, it would be foolish to attempt anything like a rival competence in an area whose experimental literature covers so many subspecialities of the natural sciences while continuously breaking boundaries with new paradigms of life research. I should also underline that nothing I say is meant to reject what is properly scientific in modern medicine, namely, how it respects nature where nature in fact appears to respond to shifting human craft and technological insights, as Jonathan Miller has shown so vividly in *The Body in Question* (1978). What a sociologist can offer as a perspective on medicalization is to show how its discoveries increasingly require us to rethink life, the individual, the family, and society. We cannot simply accommodate the new biology anymore than we do television, or the automobile, which are not easily fitted into our domestic environment without some reshaping and the growth of new dependencies (O'Neill, 2002a). In a gross way, society has housed the myriad products of the industrial process as well as its concomitant socio-political adjustments. But now we have two new instruments of modern technology capable, at the nuclear end, of destroying human society (which we shall consider in our last chapter) while promising, at the medical end, to recreate it. It is this medical promise, and what it holds out for individuals, families and the modern therapeutic state, that we must examine. In doing so, we must broaden our discussion so that it raises the larger issue of individual and civic well-being.

The practice of modern medicine is supremely technocratic and bureaucratic. Moreover, it is clean. As such, it is the envy of all other forms of managerial power in the modern administrative state; witness the extension of surgical metaphors to recent military operations. Furthermore, like the state bureaucracy itself the medical bureaucracy is self-addicting – whether public or private medicine is in question:

> the medical establishment has become a major threat to health. The depression, infection, disability and dysfunction that result from its intervention now cause more suffering than all the accidents in traffic and industry. Only the organic damage done by the industrial production of food can rival the ill-health induced by doctors. In addition, medical practice sponsors sickness by the reinforcement of a morbid society which not only industrially preserves its defectives but breeds the therapist's client in a cybernetic way. Finally, the so-called health professions have an indirect sickening power, a structurally health-denying effect. They transform pain, illness, and death from a personal challenge into a technical problem and thereby expropriate the potential of people to deal with their condition in an autonomous way. (Navarro, 1979)

The medicalization of the body is a dramatic part of the pervasive industrialization of the body observed in earlier chapters. Through it we are socialized into bringing every stage of the life cycle – conception, birth, nurturing, sexual conduct, illness, pain, aging, dying – into the administration of bureaucratized centers of professional care which weaken familized care even though it remains a residual necessity. However, we cannot continue to impose on women as quasi-natural carers nor presume upon their unpaid labor. Changes in the household economy, longevity and the interface with medicalized health/illness render home care ever more demanding. Here we might consider citizen training and payment at least in the form of income tax credits. Meantime, the hands-on care of the sick and elderly still falls to women as largely unpaid work. In part, this is because hospital practices are so costly that patient care is predicated upon high turnover and for the rest because much pain remains beyond institutional care. Of course, changes in household structures, divorce, single parenting, and the consequent strains upon intergenerationality – all place home care in jeopardy.

Just as large areas of bodily pain lie beyond the hospital, so worker alienation, occupational diseases, environmental carcinogens, chronic pain and stress, which constitute basic issues in the political economy of medicine, still have to be fully included in the dominant medical model. The sociological research finding that longevity correlates highly with work satisfaction is still passed over because of its lack of fit with the medical model of individualized diagnosis:

> In an impressive 15-year study of aging, the strongest predictor of longevity was work satisfaction. The second best predictor was overall 'happiness' … Other factors are undoubtedly important – diet, exercise, medical care and genetic inheritance. But research findings suggest that these factors may account for only about 25% of the risk factors in heart disease, the major cause of death. That is, if cholesterol, blood pressure, smoking, glucose level, serum uric acid, and so forth were perfectly controlled, only about one-fourth of coronary heart disease could be controlled. Although research on this problem has not led to conclusive answers, it appears that work role, work conditions, and other social factors may contribute heavily to this 'unexplained' 75% of risk factors. (*Work in America*, 1973: 77–9)

The extent to which the medical model trades upon very definite conceptions of the body, personality, and society for its diagnostic and treatment practices becomes clear in broad comparison with culturalist approach to well-being. The point here is not to simply propose reversing the two orders of care but to make allowance for their cooperation wherever it is appropriate (Manning and Fabrega, 1973), see Table 5.1.

Table 5.1

Objective body/self	Subjective body/self
1. physically, socially distinct	continuous, interactive
2. health/illness in either one	health/illness overlap
3. segmented role relationships	intimate, encompassing ties
4. impersonal value-free	cosmic framing of relationships
5. body/health ruled by biology	body/health more sociological than biological
6. body as a complex bio-machine	body is holistic, psycho-social
7. body is a system of highly differentiated functions	low level body system and function differentiation
8. illness/death are specifically physical/mental	illness/health are a function of social and spiritual relations
9. personality is engine of behavioral displays	personality is emergent effect of sociability
10. character traits are irrelevant to diagnosis and treatment of disease	character is a correlate of disease and cure
11. disease is independent of self-system	disease is embedded in self/society relations

Ivan Illich (1975, 1977) has argued that the medicalization of the body in Western industrial societies has reached epidemic levels. This is not, of course, an argument that we can do without medicine. Rather, the question is whether we need *as much* medicine as we have, *for whom* we have it, and *for what* we have it, and whether we should abandon all paramedical and nonmedical practices that have hitherto served to cope with and interpret the ordinary ills of embodied beings. Every day we read about unnecessary surgery, especially for women, or excessive dispensing of tranquilizers and incredibly costly prolongation of life. Here important factors are the numbers of surgeons, the nature of payment for public and private health services, and the availability of hospital beds and support staff. In exchange for the promise of expertly delivered health, people are induced to bring every stage and facet of life under clinical and hospitalized care. The medicalization of life is part of its wider industrialization whereby all ordinary human inquiry, curiosity, conflicts, relaxation, leisure, and creativity are increasingly 'problematized' in order to bring them under the 'advice' procedures of the expert lawyer, doctor, professor, counselor, or psychiatrist:

Medical Nemesis is more than all the clinical iatrogeneses put together, more than the sum of malpractice, negligence, professional callousness, political maldistribution, medically decreed disability and all the consequences of medical trial and error. It is the expropriation of man's coping ability by a maintenance service which keeps him geared up at the service of the industrial system. (Illich, 1975: 160)

The practice of medicine is clearly not examinable apart from the body politic within which it functions and upon which it may have either a helpful or an injurious effect. The nature of the intimate bond between medicine and the body politic has been subject to careful comparative study by Richard Titmuss (1971), whose arguments, while less flamboyant than those of Illich, nevertheless bear upon the fundamental principles of well-being and community (Wolstenholme, 1966). All the same, Illich's work is important if we understand it to have raised the question of how we should allocate medical resources in a society that daily makes discoveries about the inhumanity of its present market model, ruled more by dealers than healers (Etzioni, 1973).

We are living through a biomedical revolution whose aims are typically left to be decided by corporate and professional interests that are not responsible for considering the social and political consequences of their innovations. Any discussion of these issues, therefore, belongs in the public domain. The need for citizens to become involved in the new 'biosociality' (Rabinow, 1996) represents the greatest challenge to the contemporary body politic. At the same time, it raises crucial problems in political and moral education (Taviss, 1971; Holtzman, 1989).

To get a grip on the issues, I want now to follow an argument that reveals how the most profound issues of altruism and self-interest are confronted in the choice between market and nonmarket models for the collection and distribution of human blood:

> Short of examining humankind itself and the institution of slavery – of men and women as market commodities – blood as a living tissue may now constitute in Western societies one of the ultimate tests of where the 'social' begins and the 'economic' ends. If blood is considered in theory in law, and is treated in practice as a trading commodity then ultimately human hearts, kidneys, eyes and other organs of the body may also come to be treated as commodities to be bought and sold in the market place. (Titmuss, 1971: 158)

In every human community, as in every human being, blood has always been regarded as the source and symbol of life. Furthermore, human blood is surrounded with religious awe. It is the mark of life and death, of health and fertility, of holy sacrifice and unholy murder. Blood is noble when spilled in battle, awesome when menstruated. Blood is the vehicle of passion, of individual and national character. Blood, then, is both a cultural and a biomedical object. In short, whatever the strictly biological problems in thinking the production, composition, and circulation of blood, we have an equally difficult task in thinking the social production, consumption, and circulation of human blood – even more critical after the event of HIV/AIDS, as we shall see later. Of course, it is the efficacy of modern medicine that allows us to deal with the problem at all. But beyond that, we cannot understand the dimensions of the supply and demand for human blood without a knowledge of the social institutions and values which are the equivalent in the body politic of the body's internal blood system. Thus we have to have some knowledge of the development of medical techniques in which blood transfusions play a large role – from open heart surgery and transplants to Caesarian deliveries – as well as the demand for blood resulting from war, accidents, and the prolongation of life. Within the limits set by matching blood groups, the perishability of stored blood, the frequency of donations, and the necessary exclusion of certain sectors of the population (very young, very old, and known disease carriers), the potential demand for human blood seems to be limited only by the factors that bear upon the administration and distribution of its supply. In practice, there will be competition for blood among various medical sectors, giving rise to questions of priority that have to be settled either by relying more or less on market forces or by explicit planning on the lines of socialized medicine. It turns out that in fact the two options are not such clear alternatives, inasmuch as the market model seems to have deleterious effects upon the quality of the blood it collects. Titmuss's evidence shows that the market tends to collect blood from the poor and from captive populations (prisoners, students, military personnel). Often there are problems of donor health, living standards, truthfulness, and the tendency to donate too often to supplement income. Commercial collectors tend to pool blood indiscriminately and to overextend storage limits. The result is a high rate of serum hepatitis and death, particularly among patients over 40, who are the principal candidates for blood transfusions. The private market system is dangerous for both recipients and donors. Moreover, it can undermine voluntary donor systems while never being a socially adequate source of supply. Waste through spoilage, unnecessary operations, infectious diseases, and higher mortality rates must also be attributed to the market model, not to mention the social costs of commercializing attitudes toward health and life:

> From our study of the private market in blood in the United States we have concluded that the commercialization of blood and donor relationships represses the expression of altruism, erodes the sense of community, lowers scientific standards, limits both personal and professional freedoms, sanctions the making of profits in hospitals and clinical laboratories, legalizes hostility between doctor and patient, subjects critical areas of medicine to the laws of the marketplace, places immense social costs on those least able to bear them – the poor, the sick and the inept – increases the danger of unethical behaviour in various sectors of medical science and practice, and results in situations in which proportionately more and more blood is supplied by the poor, the unskilled, the unemployed, Negroes and other low income groups and categories of exploited populations of high blood yielders. Redistribution in terms of blood and blood products from the poor to the rich appears to be

one of the dominant effects of the American blood banking system. (Titmuss, 1971: 245–6)

Our consideration of the institutional contexts that affect the quality of the blood in our veins – or, as we saw earlier, our food – should be enough to convince us of the intimate ties between society, bodies, and persons, which we recollect in the metaphor of the body politic.

Actually, our earlier comments upon our meat culture should also be expanded to take account of the introduction of genetically modified crops and animals. Here, developments far exceed either visions of 'square tomatoes' grown to facilitate shipping! Even here, however, the aspiration to control size, color and taste reflects our desire to eat an industrialized order and to revise our aesthetic values in its favor. But the major reversion lies in the order of nature and culture. An industrial culture aspires to remake nature, to chemicalize its ingredients and to remove them from the spatio-temporal limits of the seasons. As well, it aspires to standardize or clone animal and human nature releasing us from natural fates:

> In the future, the new genetics will cease to be a biological metaphor for modern society and will become instead a circulation network of identity terms and restoration loci, around which and through which a truly new type of auto-production will emerge, which I call 'biosociality'. If sociobiology is culture constructed on the basis of a metaphor of nature, then biosociality nature will be modeled on culture understood as practice. Nature will be known and remade through technique and will finally become artificial, just as culture becomes natural. Were such a project to be brought to function, it would stand as the basis for overcoming the nature/culture split. (Rabinow, 1996: 99)

Consider now how similar considerations bear upon biomedical techniques for intervening in the processes of conception, fertilization, uterine control, delivery, and abortion. At the other end of life, there are technologies for live organ transplants, artificial organs, mechanical extensions of the heart, blood, and kidney systems - if not science fictions of externalized brains. We are now confronted with the growth of embryos *in vitro*, along with fundamental genetic engineering – editing – of DNA material (Olson et al., 1989). These experiments are currently viewed as the new market frontier of the biomedical sciences. Initially the customers are infertile couples, or parents seeking healthy children. Gradually the market differentiates and the customer looks for preferred timing, gender, and genetic endowment. Families, corporations, and governments may now envision orders for preferred types of human beings or for chemotherapy techniques to modify behavior, moods, and attitudes of individuals to suit institutional needs. The medicalization of the body politic is pushed from both sides – by the consumer family and by the therapeutic state and corporations. Thus a huge bioengineering industry is envisaged, built upon the raw materials of human genetics, complete with a banking system for sperm and embryos and an inventory of spare parts, to complete the industrialization of the body. We can get an idea of it all from the following snap-shot (Figure 5.1) with the understanding that the larger picture is always in the making.

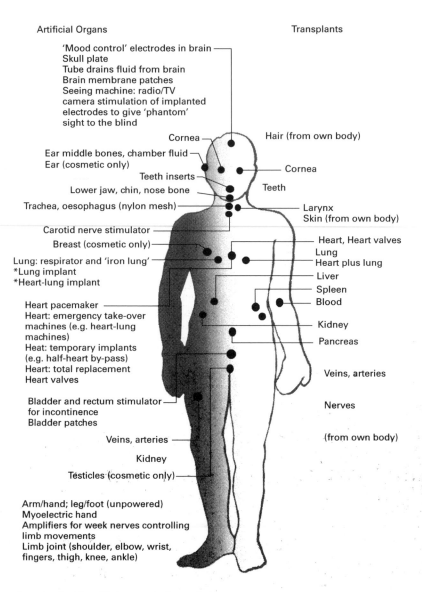

Artificial Organs   Transplants

'Mood control' electrodes in brain
Skull plate
Tube drains fluid from brain
Brain membrane patches
Seeing machine: radio/TV
camera stimulation of implanted
electrodes to give 'phantom'
sight to the blind

Cornea   Hair (from own body)

Ear middle bones, chamber fluid
Ear (cosmetic only)
                                          Cornea
Teeth inserts
Lower jaw, chin, nose bone   Teeth
Trachea, oesophagus (nylon mesh)
                                          Larynx
                                          Skin (from own body)
Carotid nerve stimulator
Breast (cosmetic only)   Heart, Heart valves
                                          Lung
Lung: respirator and 'iron lung'   Heart plus lung
*Lung implant   Liver
*Heart-lung implant   Spleen
                                          Blood
Heart pacemaker
Heart: emergency take-over
machines (e.g. heart-lung   Kidney
machines)
Heat: temporary implants   Pancreas
(e.g. half-heart by-pass)
Heart: total replacement
Heart valves   Veins, arteries

Bladder and rectum stimulator   Nerves
for incontinence
Bladder patches

Veins, arteries   (from own body)

Kidney

Testicles (cosmetic only)

Arm/hand; leg/foot (unpowered)
Myoelectric hand
Amplifiers for week nerves controlling
limb movements
Limb joint (shoulder, elbow, wrist,
fingers, thigh, knee, ankle)

* = not yet achieved in humans but expected soon

5. Spare-part man. All items other than the lung and heart-lung implants have been
achieved and are expected to have a significant clinical impact. Trivial artificial parts
such as false teeth are not included; neither are several transplant organs which
have been achieved (whole eye) or are often talked about (limbs from other bodies,
gonads) because of severe technical or ethical difficulties. Reproduced from Gerald
Leach, *The Biocrats* (London: Jonathan Cape; rpt. Penguin, 1972) by permission of
Jonathan Cape Ltd.

Figure 5.1   *Spare-part man*

It is here that the state and the market can exert the deepest influence upon the body politic, forging its genetic material, controlling its demography and social psychology. In this regard, the *prosthetic future* of the human body exists now and is not an imaginary utopia. Paradoxically, the prosthetic possibilities for redesigning the human shape raise in turn the *sociomorphic problem of the kind of society we wish to engineer*. It is here that our imagination is more likely to fail us. At the present time, conventional medicine expends incredibly fine skills on the repair of bodies that our society with its present values serves up as war, road, alcoholic, nicotine, coronary and cancer cases, not to mention the psychosomatic disorders. With existing medical resources, and assuming class differentials in access to public and private medicine, there already arise serious questions regarding medical priorities. These are not easily resolved in terms of cost-benefit analysis, since it is not easy to decide the relative value coefficients of saving lives between young and old persons, the employable and unemployable, or between the costs of caring rather than curing. It is even more difficult to estimate the difference in outcome between sociological concepts of prevention and delivery and the dominant medical model of health programs. We may ask whether biomedical engineering ought to pursue any and all of its technological possibilities (see Office of Technology Assessment, 1988). We may also ask how far society should accord individual rights of access to the potential services of biomedicine. Above all, there are enormously difficult questions concerning the agents of decision in these cases. Should decisions be made by the individual consumer, the family, the doctor, a college of physicians, hospital committees, a community or a medical parliament? Should we run medical lotteries to distribute highly expensive treatments? The questions are limitless. Do parents have a right to commit embryonic individuals to genetic xeroxing (cloning) in the service of their admiration for entertainers, politicians, sportsmen, and scientists of one kind or another? Should the state intervene to encourage or discourage individual decisions; should it have a biomedical schedule of its own? These choices can be naively conceived as an extension of consumer behavior into sperm shops, embryo banks, abortion clinics, and spare-part warehouses. Indeed, it is possible to imagine some parts of the biomedical apparatus becoming household durables as family members are plugged into various life-support machines for longer or shorter periods. Or rather, such scenarios are only conceivable provided we make unexamined assumptions about the relative places of the family medicine, and the state. One is likely to endorse the growth of biomedicine if one sees it as the servant of ordinary human dilemmas of birth, illness, and untimely death. Once one changes perspective, however, the functions of biomedicine alter. The options are usefully pictured by Etzioni (1973: 104) as follows in Table 5.2.

We need to ask how we can sustain the supreme value of individual life. I deliberately said 'individual life', rather than 'human life', in order to capture our desperately possessive concept of life. Locked into a rather short

Table 5.2   *Functions of biomedicine*

	Therapeutic goals	Breeding goals
Individual service	1.	3.
	e.g., abort deformed fetuses on demand	e.g., artificial insemination; parents' choice of donors' features
Societal service	2.	4.
Voluntary	e.g., encourage people to abort a deformed fetus	e.g., urge people to use sperm from donors who have high IQs
Coercive	e.g., require a genetic test before marriage license is issued	e.g., prohibit feeble-minded persons from marrying

biological span, confined to the reduced nuclear family contemplating childlessness in favor of consumerism, the neo-individual is obsessed with the length and physical quality of his or her life. In this concern the medical industry is a natural ally. It is there to sell better genetic material, the right child mix, physical, mental and emotional well-being, with a chance of pushing back dying and death into the realm of those brief but remediable technical failures that haunt our more sophisticated machinery:

> The Euro-American person is presented, then, as a potentially free-standing and whole entity (an individual subject or agent) contained within an abstract impersonal matrix which may include other persons but also includes other things as its context (environment/society). And this is the image of the consumer. Consumer choice is thinkable, I would suggest, precisely insofar as 'everything else' is held to lie beyond foetus/embryo/person: *anything consumed by that person comes from the outside*, whether or not the source is other persons. For generative power lies in the individual person's own desire for experience. Desire and experience: the principal dimensions of the consumer's relationship with his/her environment. And the field is infinite; it consists of the sum of all the possibilities that may be sampled. Satisfied from without, the impetus is held to spring from within. While individual desires may be stimulated by the outside world – advertising, marketing and so forth – that in turn is supposed to be oriented to the consumer's wants.
>
> Whereas the Melanesian capacity to receive has to be nurtured in and elicited from a partner, sometimes to the point of coercion, the twentieth-century consumer is depicted as having infinite appetite. Above all, the consumer is a consumer of experience and thus of him-/herself. Perhaps it is against the compulsion of appetite, the coercion of having to choose, the prescriptiveness of subjective self-reference, that the possibility of unbidden goods and unanticipated experiences presents itself as exotic. The 'free gift'. (Strathern, 1992: 135)

The medicalization of the body, as Titmuss observes, requires once again that we learn to demarcate *civic economy of altruism* in which we learn once again that we are social bodies. At the heart of every social system there lies the *reciprocal* gift – the exchange that binds people together for the sake of everything and anything else that they may undertake. The market is ill pre-pared to serve the body politic in respect of the new economy of biomedical artifacts, operations, and exchanges. Thus the gift of blood has no price; it must be rich; it cannot be withheld. Its availability is the mark of a charitable society; its collection and distribution articulates the anonymous love of that society's members toward their strangers. The circulation of blood is, therefore, socially speaking just as vital to the life of the ethical community as it is to the life of the individual. Moreover, as Titmuss says, what can be said of blood circulation applies in every detail to the social organization of the more exotic prosthetics of biomedicine:

> The ways in which society organizes and structures its social institutions – and particularly its health and welfare systems – can encourage or discourage the altruistic in man; such systems can foster integration or alienation; they can allow the 'theme of the gift' (to recall Mauss's words) – of generosity towards strangers – to spread among and between social groups and generations. This ... is an aspect of freedom in the twentieth century which, compared with the emphasis on consumer choice in material aquisitiveness, is insufficiently recog-nized. It is indeed little understood how modern society, technical, profes-sional, large-scale organized society – allows few opportunities for ordinary people to articulate giving in morally practical terms outside their own network of family and personal relationships. (Titmuss, 1971: 225–6)

Titmuss's worry that our health system may be undermining civic partici-pation as a life-affirming value raises a profound question regarding the gifts of community and solidarity in the circulation of the gift of life. This ques-tion becomes even more urgent when we set it in the context of the global economy of life and death. We have recast world history so that it appears to us as a story designed to celebrate and to legitimate our colonial inter-vention in all 'earlier' (older) societies whose technology was less industri-alized, less militarized and less medicalized than our own, and whose conquest we now offer to redeem with charitable impositions of technical, medical and military 'aid'. Let us 'map' the *prosthetic mythology* that has underwritten the double narrative of historical (technological) develop-ment and social (ethical) progress, see Figure 5.2.

Thus we may represent our history through two moments of decisive transformation in the body's relationship to its world, determined by its inscription in a colonial history of modernization. The mapping of the two bodily events, AID and AIDS, is to be read as a contrastive economy of domination and emancipation, in which the exchange of 'milk' and 'blood' symbolizes two embodied operators in an economy of the gift that must be 'good' if society is to endure. In other words, in a preindustrial society the social bond may be rendered through the maternal icon – the good gift of the mother's milk – while in an industrial society the social bond may be rendered in terms of the medicalized gift of blood. Because the gift of blood is necessarily transferred by a medical technology, whereas the gift of milk

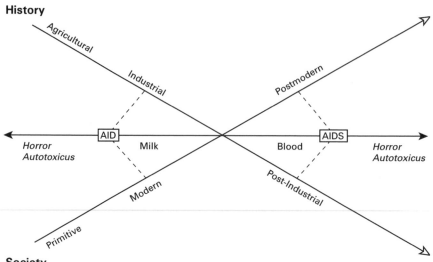

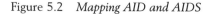

Figure 5.2   *Mapping AID and AIDS*

is not, we may mark the colonization of milk societies through such prosthetic devices as bottle-feeding.

The power of modern industrial society over itself and its natural environment generates *a myth of auto-immunity*, which society acts out in endless medical interventions upon itself. These are specularized, for example, in medical soap operas and in documentaries of medicalized 'aid' to 'underdeveloped' countries whose overwhelming hunger and disease weaken their immunity to political and economic conquest. Western medicine saves these countries from themselves and from other political predators. This conception of things, of course, hides the earlier destruction of non-Western medical practices by colonial medicine (Melrose, 1982). The latter intervention is most succinctly dramatized in the African mother who abandons breastfeeding in favor of bottle-feeding in response to the iconology of modernization and medical progress (Van Esterik, 1989). But, the scarcity and unpredictable supply of the milk formula increasingly oblige the mother – who has stopped lactating – to dilute the formula with water so contaminated that she would not otherwise have given it to her infant. The result is that she slowly starves and poisons her own child in the most horrific inscription of maternal love and modernity. The cure here, unfortunately, involves the complete modernization of the social infrastructures presupposed by Western medical practices. 'Health' is sought at the expense of both native and communal medical institutions and through dependence within its political economy and on the diseases it globalizes. Thus nothing represents the postmodern moment in our history more sharply than the transformation of our sexuality in its encounter with the HIV virus. Let us set aside initial attempts to draw a line between heterosexuals and homosexuals, between IV drug-users and nonusers or between 'first' and 'third' worlds. In a blood society, two communities cannot be separated into two immunosystems, one 'outside' of, or ghettoized by, the other. Yet, in the context of the global order, the 'first world' at first toyed with the construction of a political epidemiology in which its internal Third World of Blacks and Hispanics were 'objectively' identified as the principal threat to White America's immune system. Moreover, the same 'map' was deployed to track the 'African' origins of HIV whose transmission followed the trade routes of commerce and war (O'Neill, 1990).

Despite the contemporary celebrations of endless exchange value, we cannot abandon the idea of use value. But 'use' must mean 'good enough' to serve its purpose and thereby to earn a similarly well-produced return. The gifts of milk and blood are not good because they are exchanged, but are exchanged because they are good, for society and for posterity. Life is doubled from the standpoint of collective and intergenerational circulation. All gifts are ecogifts – that is 'eco' from *oikos*, as 'source of sustainable life' – or better, they are maintainable goods to which we have right of production as well as a duty of consumption. Hence milk and blood society – and water, air, 'green' – are garnishes of the sacred. 'Sacred' means not appropriable (in mimetic rivalry) because life ought not to be opposed to itself – but repeated here and there – parochially, *per omnia saecula saeculorum*. Therefore, what is secular is not opposed to what is sacred. Rather the 'secular' is what is given to be continued, to be repeated and be reproduced within the fold of the sacred. The 'sacred' marks off the clearing, the lightning space, in which it here can be a civil domain and from which all other human institutions arise. The sacred is not a vision of things beyond what lies before us; it is the vision that discerns the very realm of thought, an appropriation of reality according to a language whose own history will differentiate the realms of law, science, economy, art and literature, but from an original matrix of poetry and fable, as Vico demonstrated in *The New Science* ([1744] 1970).

Any consideration of global health – since that is the ultimate direction of our concerns – cannot ignore the global spread of industrial contamination that destroys the capacity of nature to become a culture. Hitherto, the function of myth was to reveal the dialectic of reciprocity between society and nature, between cleanness and dirt, civil and savage, male and female, between the human and the monstrous. To the extent that industrial societies destroy nature's capacity to become culture, we naturalize our own culture – but at the level of a barbarism from which our myths had once delivered us. The zero point of civilization looms once neither nature nor culture can no longer produce *the good gift*, where civilization is ruled by incontinence and indifference, where nothing is sacrificed to limit, exchange and the double legacy of present and future generation.

Today the failure of modernism divides us into celebrants and fundamentalists. Each side will characterize the other according to its own wit. But it will be difficult for either side to ground its own wit in sound institutions. Such is the predicament of postmodernity: the fundamentalists will invoke an arcadian moment and the necessary return to the harmony of nature and the human body as the guarantee of any future history, while the celebrants will find nature in a zoo, or in an arcade, where they hunt themselves in video games of digital death. Whether we survive our new barbarism will depend on whether blood societies can restore what is sacred in the gift they still borrow.

6

Conclusion

The Future Shape of Human Beings

Our situation, as we have considered it in the light of our potential for revising the very status of life, requires us to think of all technology as biotechnology – to see that *every power over nature is a power over ourselves*. Bio-power is not only present in our machines but proliferates in the discursive production of the human sciences designed to control life, health, sanity, and knowledge. An escalation of this power occurs once the bio-therapeutic state discovers that the will to knowledge can be conscripted to redesign the beginnings and ends of life and to administer its course (Haraway, 1997). Of course, society has always shaped life, as I have tried to show throughout this work. But we appear now to stand on a frontier where the origins and ends of life converge, making us more of a question for ourselves than ever before.

If today's humanists are to have any say in the future shaping of human beings, they must take their stand on the alpha and omega questions. They must, in other words, be concerned with the future shaping of life and death – and therefore of the future of kinship:

> For the European anthropologist, the concept of culture is already problematised. It is not at all clear what is or is not an artefact. The point is not that the boundaries between bodies and machines are theoretically troublesome … The particular pair (body, machine) were formerly connected and contrasted by analogy, in that they provided metaphors for different aspects of human nature. It is their metaphorical status that now seems subject to encroachment. Technology literally helps 'life' to 'work'. No doubt people will go on talking about assisting nature in the same way as they talk of releasing engineered life-forms 'into' an environment that they have already altered. Yet insofar as they cannot evoke distinctive domains of life, bodies and machines can no longer serve as metaphors for one another. It follows that the relation between them will become a poor analogy for contrasting what is given in the world with what is artificial, the basis upon which the anthropological concept of culture has rested throughout the twentieth century. It is not the challenge to the substantive concept that must be of most interest to anthropology, but the challenge to the conventional facility to draw analogies. (Strathern, 1992: 60)

This means, as I have tried to show, that civic humanists cannot ignore the import of current state and social policy upon the design of life, sexuality, and family constitution. With regard to these questions, we stand in a landscape as wild as that in which Vico's first human beings once stood, listening for the lightning sounds from which they shaped the world's earliest poem, thereby giving to their awkward bodies the human shape of familied society:

> And because in such a case the nature of the human mind leads it to attribute its own nature to the effect, and because in that state their nature was that of men all of robust bodily strength, who expressed their very violent passions by shouting and grumbling, they pictured the sky to themselves as a great animated body, which in that aspect they called Jove, the first god of the so-called greater gentes, who meant to tell them something by the hiss of his bolts and the clap of his thunder. And thus they began to exercise that natural curiosity which is the daughter of ignorance and the mother of knowledge, and which, opening the mind of man, gives birth to wonder. (Vico, 1970, para. 377)

Whatever their ingenuity, all later thinkers stand in a necessary historical line from the first human creatures whose awkward bodies ruled them as the generative source of our metaphors, relationships, concepts, and generalizations. This is the historical ground of common sense considered as an achievement that is fundamental to any higher unity of humankind.

Just as the first humans were called upon to think the world with their bodies, today we must once again rethink society, kinship and history with our bodies. We must do so in order to restore the lost shape of our humanity which we portray to ourselves in cyborgs, ghosts, and talking dolls while pretending a civilized distance between such mutants and ourselves. What is at stake is not only love and marriage but the survival of children, of intergenerationality, of kinship. The law of family is no different from the law of any other institution. But to the isolate, family will appear to be an extra-terrestrial message. Thus Elliot's replacement of his father with E.T. the extra-terrestrial as a surrogate 'brother' makes Elliot his own mother/father by creating E.T. from himself [E(llio)T]. His challenge to his mother that Dad would believe him (whereas she doubts his fantasy), in part reasserts the patrilineage he acts out when alone, playing Dad with a beer, newspaper and television. But, Elliot's invention of E.T. also teaches the lesson in (or of) the father's absence – that one's home is where one learns to relinquish the parent in exchange for an independent imagination. The question remains whether the ideologies of the larger society have scrambled the family message while hoping our children will decode it for us. This cultural indecision with respect to the goodness/evil of our institutions will be played out in any number of scenarios. The state, the corporation, the law, the police, science, sexuality, women and children will all be cast as good/bad figures. We will similarly split our conservatism/liberalism, collectivism and individualism, ourselves and our robots, opposing our creativeness to our creatureliness, as we do in the hybrid figures of science fiction whose alien visitors are likely to be benevolent, messianic figures or malevolent and evil. Like the very figure of E.T., they represent what is indecisive about our techno-future. This indecision is deepened, for example, in *Blade Runner* (1982) where the line between the human and the android shifts over into the line between good/bad replicants to whom we have left a legacy of urban garbage and corrosive rain falling on what was once the city of angels (Los Angeles). Here survival of our humanity rests with its trace behavior (sympathy, memory, kinship) in Roy who sacrifices himself to save Deckard who may love Rachel, happily recycled ever after. The logic of waste is that waste is needed to recycle waste. The endless semiotic repetitions and citations that serve the hallucinatory projection of place, buildings, language, identity and emotion in L.A.

We must learn like Vico's giants how to 'phone home'. Therefore, I want now to propose the following construct, a piece of historical bricolage that may seem even more crude than E.T.'s desperate device. I want to join the embodied history of the first humans to the disembodied history of today's world. I wish to join the first appearance of our humanity to the present disappearance of our own kind as we may see it in passages I shall take from *Time*, the sociologist's poor Homer and the egg-story in the film, *Jurassic Park* (1993). In 1982, according to *Time*, 'the man of the year' was a machine. The magazine's cover for January 3, 1983 was devoted to the computer, celebrating that machine's invasion of America. Inside was a story of a second invasion of the American home and heartland, this one by the film *E.T.: The Extra-Terrestrial* (1982) E.T. is certainly not a machine, nor a man nor a woman. Like many a man and woman, however, 'he' seems to be a displaced person. Only children – and accompanying adults – understand him, uncertain as both are of their own kind in a world where innocence and friendship are made alien.

Our children already know that our cyborgs are at war between themselves and sometimes with us. We are unsure of the virtues of virtual reality. We are leery of runaway machines, identities, sexualities, of electronic wombs that expand our monsters. In this mood our future darkens and our intergalactic imagination has already collapsed amidst the endless debris of past wars, past crimes and past vices that return with the impunity of experience from which we might otherwise patiently sieve our future. Everything enjoys obsolescence once there is nothing in which we believe. Thus we ourselves become cultural throwaways and are only able to retrieve our antique selves in the nostalgia of recycling and heritage retrospectives. To this extent, we are stalled in the cooling of history which Baudrillard (1994) speaks, referring to the endless cancellation of human events once we abandon any truly millennial hope of the fulfillment of human time. Yet it may also be claimed that we are already launched as cyborgs (Haraway, 1991) and that our future is one of endless cybermorphosis. In other words, we are becoming some third creature of communications technology and of bio-technology, very like the UK Millennial Madonna herself, see Figure 6.1.

Our cyborg futures hold out the prospect of a conquest of genetic and viral risks, and of a productive by-pass that will wipe out the sociological viruses of heterosexuality and inequality. By cyborging ourselves, we hope to erase the hard lines between life and death, between male and female,

Figure 6.1   *Millennial Madonna*

between science and fiction; we hope to erase the line between origins and ends, between animals and machines, between fiction and reality. Above all, cyborgs are indifferent to the lines between class, race, gender, and in this sense, launch our hopes and anxieties into the next millennium. Yet we are not absolutely sure that we shall succeed in third-kind recombinations of ourselves floating in cyberspace, unhinged from everyday engagements of personal and social life. We suspect that virtual empowerment is solipsistic and that it borders on the psychotic. Its risk is the disillusionment involved in the discovery that cyberspace is after all a transitional space. Its revision-ing of the personal and the political, as Plato already told us, must be brought out of the sunlight into the everyday world of character and com-munity where time and its endurance are our lot:

> Was there a time when dancers with their fiddles
> In children's circuses could stay their troubles?
> There was a time they could cry over books,
> But time has set its maggot on their track
> Under the arc of the sky they are unsafe.
> What's never known is safest in this life.
> Under the skysigns they who have no arms
> Have cleanest hands, and, as the heartless ghost
> Alone's unhurt, so the blind man sees best.

(Dylan Thomas, 1952: 50)

The computer and E.T. represent two ways of reflecting upon the future shape of human beings – two modes of extra-territoriality that bring into focus the challenge that faces the human imagination in the modern world. As we look to our future, the life of science, and not only of the life sciences, is sure to be invoked as the highest conception we have of ourselves. This view is likely to prevail because we now conceive life itself as the very elemental structure of communication, the DNA code. Biotechnology must currently be seen in terms of two prosthetic strategies, one now largely available, and the other increasingly possible:

1 *spare-part prosthetics*
2 *genetic prosthetics*

The two strategies represent a shift from the exo-design of spare-part 'man' to the endo-design of *prosthetic life*. Although seemingly on the same biomedical frontier, the two projects are as far apart as the stages of early and late capitalism. The economy of spare-part prosthetics involves us in a combination of medical craft and commercial banking and distribution procedures. Such systems may be entrepreneurially or state managed, and both may draw upon voluntary donors. As we saw earlier, Titmuss has shown that, in the case of blood transfusion systems, a number of problems with quality and continuity arise when the spare-part supply depends on commercial rather than voluntary services. In the long run the problems of the spare-part economy may be circumvented whenever it becomes possible to anticipate genetic faults and to correct them at the DNA level. To the extent that such genetic engineering is possible – and its immediate potential should not be exaggerated – we might then implant the basic market rationality of efficiency and choice at the very DNA level. Thus, we now contemplate parental choice of biologically perfect embryos. A mark of such perfection, from the point of view of parents, would consist in the embryonic replication (cloning) of themselves or of their social idols. Once these possibilities emerge, then biotechnology will finally deliver the myth of Narcissus from its mirror. It will defamilize the body and the imagination of future individuals, making them the creatures of the dominant ethos of the *market or the state as matrix*. Under such conditions, the institution of life, and not only its bioconstitution, will be radically altered. In the laboratory and the clinic, life no longer has any history. Birth will become a consumer fiction, like Mother's Day. Thereafter our hitherto embodied and familied histories will float in a commercial narcosis monopolized by an entrepreneurial or statist biocracy, or what Rose calls *ethopolitics*:

> Biopolitics, here, merges with what I have termed 'ethopolitics': the politics of life itself and how it should be lived (Rose, 1999). By ethopolitics I mean to characterize ways in which the ethos of human existence – the sentiments, moral nature or guiding beliefs of persons, groups, or institutions – have come to provide the 'medium' within which the self-government of the autonomous individual can be connected up with the imperatives of good government. In ethopolitics, life itself, as it is lived in its everyday manifestations, is the object of adjudication. If discipline individualizes and normalizes, and biopower collectivizes and socializes, ethopolitics concerns itself with the self-techniques by which human beings should judge themselves and act upon themselves to

> make themselves better than they are. While ethopolitical concerns range from those of lifestyle to those of community, they coalesce around a kind of vital-ism: disputes over the value to be accorded to life itself: 'quality of life', 'the right to life' or 'the right to choose', euthanasia, gene therapy, human cloning and the like. (Rose, 2001: 18)

The emancipation of the human family from the biology of the Bible is the last stage of Prometheanism. The death of the father waits in the psyche and in language for the death of the mother achieved in the biosciences. The death of God involves a double murder. It is not only that sons must kill the father and steal his knowledge for the gift of science. Daughters, too, must murder, silencing the womb, floating life in a petri dish, gift of the bio-sciences. The new geneticism completes the end of patriarchy. Sperm bank-ing and quality control will dominate sperm production, rendering obsolete the current ideologies of dephallicization and feminism because they have no control over the biomaterial selection of life. The advent of the bio-genetic identity card, however, raises once again the question of the rela-tions between power and desire. Once desire is merely the exhausted image of an obsolete species, power solidifies without fear that we shall refuse to imprint upon it. Love finally becomes an illness without any trace of divi-nity, knowledge is severed from information, and memory is exhausted by retrieval systems. No law opposes this because there is no longer any sub-ject of knowledge, no longer any subject of desire, no transgression. The law will have been entirely absorbed by the ownership of the means of com-munication. It cannot be opposed by its clones because each is the same and each incapable of forming relations of opposition.

The good news of geneticism is that only the computerized intelligence capable of practicing DNA eugenics upon itself can master the biblical chaos. The birth of biotechnology promises a second genesis to which we will owe the re-creation of ourselves and our food chain – all in the name of better living. It is therefore imperative to maximize the spectacle of *in vitro* fertilization, surrogate pregnancy, and transplantation, as well as the new animal and plant genetics that will complete the industrialization of nature through the capture of its information codes. No one notices that soon as many people will be required to launch a baby as are now required to launch a satellite! If obsolescence kills future time in order to bring child-hood closer to adulthood, the paleo-renaissance kills past time in order to bring adulthood even closer to childhood. This double strategy of time col-lapse and the consequent erasure of intergenerationality is necessary in order to subject history to empty time and thereby to reduce the history of mind to the instant recovery of factoids. For this temporal strategy to suc-ceed, it is also necessary that the content of human history be reduced to its simulacra so that the events of history are entirely consumed by their replay. This in turn permits the complete externalization of culture and history, so that our experience can be set forward and backward at will.

In *Jurassic Park* (1993) the primal scene is transposed to the scene of primeval birth – the splitting of the dino-egg witnessed by the paleo-family,

Ellie, Allen, Lexis, and Tim. Here the children are attendants to a wildlife birth that is entirely induced by the unnatural history of *JP*'s geneticism and its crazy scheme of superovulation. To celebrate their future the new foundlings must attend the spectacle of the past's reanimation – the new Easter of the dino-egg fertilized by the marriage of science and commerce. *JP* is the Bethlehem of bioscientism and a renewed biorevolution. Here all children are summoned to witness the rebirth of the struggle for life and the survival of the computerized fit. Here is proclaimed the end of mammalian humanity powerless against brutes and terrified into divinity. Worse still, the embryo is confused with an egg to be found in the supermarket or at TOYS-R-US. More like a gum-ball than an egg, dinovum is, however, the perfectly atomic origin of the individual conceived without social relations. Thus the extrafamilial egg fulfills the fantasy of an aboriginal choice of life. The price of the choice is the interchangeability of the raw material of humanity, bringing DNA into the same market where human labor still struggles with the gap between the sovereignty of consumption and the servitude of production. Here history repeats itself. Just as labor was discovered to be 'inefficient' (it built the cathedral of Chartres, the Taj Mahal, and the Stradivarius, as well as the great roads, bridges, and ships of the world), so human sexuality is now discovered to lack quality control and even to be fraught with sterility.

The potential infertility of Ellie and Alan's relationship is doubly increased by the contemporary loss of family authority and by the substitute authority of the procreativity of the biosciences. Here the death wish of the American family is fed by life wish of the sciences that promise to underwrite individualism and consumerism. In a future where science can make babies, we shall no longer need to subordinate enjoying ourselves to (re)producing ourselves. Here the only risk to consumer sovereignty is the usual one of restriction of brands/clones in favor of efficiency and profitability – in short, the risk that our own person may not sell well and be removed from the DNA strip. However, the positive fancy in bio-shopping should also be addressed if we are to understand the perennial attraction of the amusement park as a Garden of Eden in which we get to make all the animals – even if they and ourselves are only toy animals. In short, there is in the story an infantile fantasy of bypassing the primal scene of reproduction through a combination of lab, computer, and art skills that the superkid can master, renewing human history as a game run by and for children.

As we move into an age where the origins and ends of life are increasingly recast in the marriage of biology and technology, the mystery of life may one day surrender to the clinical vision of our laboratories. Once our bodies are entirely machine-readable, we may embark on a new edition of the human text. Meanwhile, by means of the telephone and the telescope, by writing and lodging, we have left nature's womb forever. In the distance created by our future biotechnologies, we may one day erase our maternal memory and with it the world's great model of love. Yet beneath the fantasy of the new geneticism, we may sense old-order questions. Who am I?

Why am I? What am I to do? My parents are not my parents – they are DNA shoppers; my mother was not my mother – her mother was to help her out; my sex is not my sex – it is the sex picked for those who bought me. I am the child of the end of the family. Henceforth I shall be ruled by conjugal convenience rather than the family romance. Henceforth I shall not need to think myself but rather to keep up with the fashions in the biomarket, in the market schools, and in the marketplace. Henceforth I am both omnipotent child and the impotent child. The genetic primal scene requires no self-discovery beyond a bare look into the microscope. No life stories emerge beyond the history of one's biorepairs. The end of childhood.

I turn now to life at the other end. Despite contemporary atrocities, we consider that in the West we have progressively made death more 'humane.' The gallows, the guillotine, the gas chamber, the electric chair have all been considered stages in the humanity of death by execution. In December 1982, a new height was reached when a lethal injection of a mixture of sodium thiopental, pancuronium bromide, and potassium chloride was administered to Charles Brooks in a Texas prison. *Time* magazine noted that there was 'nothing new' in Brook's medicalized execution, since Socrates seems to have had first claim to hemlock. The appeal to efficiency and reasonableness of punishment has a long history in the enlightened human sciences. The medicalization of the practice of execution appears thus to be the last stage in the humanity of death. It permits us to believe that the disciplinary and punitive order required by our collective life might be exercised as an act of individual love and subjectivized care. To date, medicalized executions are not a general practice. However, should the death penalty be restored outside of America, one can expect this rationale for it to be invoked. We may expect it because medicalization (with the addition of implants to facilitate surveillance) is a general feature in the practice of managing deviants, insane, clinically hospitalized, and imprisoned populations. Pharmacological therapies are widespread practices both inside and outside these institutions. Self-administered drugs – the so-called nonmedical uses – are part of the same complex whereby individuals are treated, or treat themselves, as the troubled agents of society. Indeed, the tranquilizing of citizens (and children) is the most distinctive feature of the modern therapeutic society. It is the hallmark of our medicalized humanity. From birth to death, in school, work, prison, and play we can expect to be drugged in order to preserve the dream of secularized happiness in a world unable to deliver its reality. Psychotropically induced tranquility is a marvelous irony of modern life. It bespeaks the determination to be in control while out of control, to be calm in a state of crisis. Drug use makes the mind the prison of the body in a terrible reversal of the terms of ancient morality. The intervening mechanism is the creation of a society that claims to dominate nature while so many of its members are powerless and out of touch with their own nature. Thus the great human events of birth, labor, marriage, and death are removed from our humanity in the name of our modernity, which experiences its liturgical moments as medicalized, pharmacological events tied to the professional practice of administered care.

In the same issue of *Time* that reported Charles Brooks's medicalized death (December 20, 1982: 52–5), there is the story of Barney Clark's experience with the implantation of an artificial heart, Jarvik-7, an event marred only by his home having been vandalized in his absence. Here we have the heroic end of medicine extending life – or death – for 112 days, displacing malfunctioning organs. The social and ideological investment in the success of these practices is huge, and overdetermines the drama of intimate fates. The Barney Clark story is immediately followed by an account of genetic 'surgery' employing recombinant-DNA techniques to replace 'bad' genes with 'good' genes to improve the quality of life. The Show Business section carries the story of *Tootsie* – 1982's most celebrated anthropomorphosis. In this film an unsuccessful male actor, Michael Dorsey finds success as Dorothy Michaels, coming to the (offstage?) conclusion: 'I was a better man as a woman with a woman than I've been as a man with a woman.' In the Behavior Section, we then find a report called 'The Hollowing of America,' in which the crippling effects of narcissism upon the family, school, and workplace are deplored. It would seem that none of these issues should escape our attention. Somehow they either challenge 'basic values', which might lead us deplore them, or else they provoke a more profound grasp of the future shape of human beings of which they are the portent. But, sadly, *Time* has no time to construct the interpretive framework of historical and structural analysis that I have required of the reader to this point.

Time, then, destroys our memory by keeping us up to date, just as it disorients us by keeping us in touch with the world viewed from America. In its fast food format we encounter the difference between the embodied time and family of common-sense knowledge and the implosive tempo of information that makes us obsolescent the more we are addicted to it. If social scientists have a Homer or Virgil, it cannot by now be much more than their daily readings of the press and television (O'Neill, 2002b). In keeping with such practice, I have culled from *Time* a small sample of events that reveal how the human shaping of human beings is a feature of our everyday lives and not an utterly remote utopia of morality and medicine. In conclusion, I shall keep within the philosophical limits of the *Time* essay – 'Do Not Go Gentle Into That Good Night'. In a remarkable page, Roger Rosenblatt muses on the irony of the medical inventiveness employed respectively in the case of Brooks and of Clark, one to die, the other to live. Rosenblatt is rightly puzzled by the civilizing intentions behind each operation, unable to balance the hope in one case against the despair in the other. What obsesses him is the removal of the executioner's deed from public view. Even though there was a death watch for Charlie Brooks, the medical execution did not show itself; it did not write itself upon the body as our collective deed. Nor did it, some twenty years later, when the 'Oklahoma Bomber', Timothy McVeigh, was executed – despite calls for televising the execution in America's post 9/11 rage for revenge. Here the sociotext erases any trace of the biotext, putting the administration of Brooks's death beyond our humanity. Rosenblatt appears to be pleading for a public death, for a restoration of the theater of life and death in which we can be restored to the sacrificial sense of our own good and evil. Unlike the Cross or the Star of David, the photos and magazine sketches that trace Brooks's death leave us with no acceptable icon of human suffering. The medical sleep erases the epiphany of death and our remembrance of life. Here, then, with the poet we must cry:

> Do not go gentle into that good night
> Old age should burn and rave at close of day
> Rage, rage against the dying of the light.
> Though wise men at their end know dark is right,
> Because their words had forked no lightning they
> Do not go gentle into that good night.
> Good men, the last wave by, crying how bright
> Their frail deeds might have danced in a green bay,
> Do not go gentle into that good night.
> Wild men who caught and sang the sun in flight,
> And learn, too late, they grieved it on his way,
> Do not go gentle into that good night.
> (Dylan Thomas, 1952: 116)

Time's reportage cannot exceed the standstill of contemporary events whose uniform reproduction deprives them of any aura or transcendental reach (Benjamin, 1973: 171). The metaphysics of journalism are severed from daily prayer; sense is lost in sensation and meaning is consumed by presentation. The paradox of the speechlessness of the age of communication derives from the materiality of its representation of a world where sense is stalled between a reasonableness and non-sense. Modernity now suspends both idealism and its materialism because it has no vision of an end to its death toll.

Today we are threatened with the prospect of an eternal darkness that may burst upon us from those burning suns we toy with turning against ourselves. Truly we are living in a dry season, unsure that anything will take root, sap, and bloom; and cannot tell our children otherwise, nor any god. Born naked, modern humanity risks dying without the mask of culture, destroyed by impulses that suffer no cultural interdiction. In the meantime, we continue to violate the good differences within humanity with the bad differences of class, racism and imperial power. Unable to see ourselves in these practices, we may yet do so in the crack of nature's mirror before which we once more stand as the world's barbarians.

Bibliography

Archambault, Paul (1967) 'The analogy of the "body" in Renaissance political literature', *Bibliothèque d'Humanisme et Renaissance*, 29: 21–63.

Baldwin, B.A. (1974) 'Behavioural thermoregulation,' in J.I. Monteith and L.E. Mount (eds), *Heat Loss from Animals and Man: Assessment and Control*. London: Butterworth.

Baran, Paul A. (1969) *The Longer View: Essays toward a Critique of Political Economy*. Ed. with an introduction by John O'Neill. New York: Monthly Review Press.

Barkan, Leonard (1975) *Nature's Work of Art: The Human Body as Image of the World*. New Haven, CT: Yale University Press.

Barthes, Roland (1973) *Mythologies*. Selected and tran. Annette Lavette. London: Paladin.

Baudrillard, Jean (1972) *Pour une critique de l'économie politique du signe*. Paris: Gallimard.

Baudrillard, Jean (1979) *De la séduction*. Paris: Galilée.

Baudrillard, Jean (1994) *The Illusion of God*. Oxford: Polity Press.

Benedict, Ruth (1935) *Patterns of Culture*. London: Routledge & Kegan Paul.

Benjamin, Walter (1973) *Charles Baudelaire: A Lyric Poet in the Era of High Capitalism*. London: NLB.

Berman, Morris (1981) *The Reenchantment of the World*. Ithaca, NY: Cornell University Press.

Blake, William (1982) *The Complete Prose and Poetry of William Blake*, newly revised edition, ed. David V. Erdman. Berkeley, CA: University of California Press.

Bledstein, Burton J. (1978) *The Culture of Professionalism: The Middle Class and the Development of Higher Education in America*. New York: Norton.

Bologh, Roslyn Wallach (1979) *Dialectical Phenomenology: Marx's Method*. London: Routledge & Kegan Paul.

Borgstrom, George (1973) *The Food and People Dilemma*. Belmont, CA: Duxbury Press.

Bourdieu, Pierre (1977) 'Remarques provisoires sur la perception sociale du corps', *Actes de la Recherche en Sciences Sociales*, April 14: 51–4.

Brophy, Julia and Smart, Carol (1981) 'From disregard to disrepute: the position of women in family law', *Feminist Review*, 9: 3–15.

Bulmer, Ralph (1967) 'Why is the cassowary not a bird? A problem of zoological taxonomy among the Karam of the New Guinea Highlands', *Man*, n.s. 2 (March): 5–25.

Busaca, Richard, and Ryan, Mary P. (1982) 'Beyond the family crisis', *Democracy*, 2 (Fall): 79–92.

Calame-Griaule, Geneviève (1965) *Ethnologie et langue: La parole chez les Dogon*. Paris: Gallimard.

Caplan, Arthur L (1978) *The Sociobiology Debate*. New York: Harper & Row.

Clark, Carole (1970) 'Montaigne and the imagery of political discourse in sixteenth century France', *French Studies*, 24: 337–55.

Cockburn, Alexander (1977) 'Gastro-porn', *The New York Review of Books*, December 8: 15–19.

Conger, George Perrigo (1922) *Theories of Macrocosms and Microcosms*. New York: Columbia University Press.

Cooley, Charles Horton (1964) *Human Nature and the Social Order*. New York: Schocken.

Cox, Harvey (1971) *The Secular City: Secularization and Urbanization in Theological Perspective*. New York: Macmillan.

Crawford, M.A. and Rivers, J.P.W. (1975) 'The protein myth', in E. Steele and A. Bourne (eds), *The Mani Food Equation*. New York: Academic Press.

Davis, Nanette J. and Anderson, Bo (1983) *Social Control: The Production of Deviance in the Modern State*. New York: Irvington.

Diener, Paul, and Robkin, Eugene E. (1978) 'Ecology, evolution, and the search for cultural origins: the question of Islamic pig production', *Current Anthropology*, 19: 493–540.

Donzelot, Jacques (1979) *The Policing of Families*. Tran. Robert Hurley. New York: Pantheon.

Douglas, Mary (1970) *Purity and Danger: An Analysis of Concepts of Pollution and Taboo*. Harmondsworth: Penguin Books.

Douglas, Mary (1973) *Natural Symbols: Explorations in Cosmology*. Harmondsworth: Penguin.

Douglas, Mary (1975) *Implicit Meanings: Essays in Anthropology*. London: Routledge & Kegan Paul.

Douglas, Mary (1978) *Cultural Bias*. Occasional Paper no. 35. London: Royal Anthropological Institute of Great Britain and Ireland.

Douglas, Mary and Isherwood, Baron (1979) *The World of Goods: Towards an Anthropology of Consumption*. London: Allen Lane.

Durkheim, Emile and Mauss, Marcel (1963) *Primitive Classification*. Tran. and ed. with an introduction by Rodney Needham. London: Cohen & West.

Eliade, Mircea (1978) *The Forge and the Crucible: The Origins and Structures of Alchemy*. Tran. Stephen Corrin. 2nd edn. Chicago: University of Chicago Press.

Elias, Norbert (1978) *The Civilizing Process*. Vol. 1 *The History of Manners*. Oxford: Basil Blackwell.

Elshtain, Jean Bethke (1981) *Public Man, Private Woman: Women in Social and Political Thought*. Oxford: Martin Robertson.

Esping-Andersen, Gosta (1990) *The Three Worlds of Welfare Capitalism*. Oxford: Polity Press.

Etzioni, Amitai (1973) *Genetic Fix: The Next Technological Revolution*. New York: Harper Colophon.

Ewen, Stuart (1976) *Captains of Consciousness: Advertising and the Social Roots of the Consumer Culture*. New York: McGraw-Hill.

Fortescue, Sir John (1942) *De Laudibus Legum Angliae*. Ed. and tran. with introduction and notes by S.B. Chrimes. Cambridge: Cambridge University Press.

Foucault, Michel (1979) *Discipline and Punish: The Birth of the Prison*. Tran. Alan Sheridan. New York: Vintage.

Foucault, Michel (1980) *The History of Sexuality*. Vol. 1. *An Introduction*. New York: Viking Books.

Freud, Sigmund (1962) *Civilization and Its Discontents*. Tran. and ed. James Strachey. New York: Norton.

Frosch, Thomas R (1974) *The Awakening of Albion: The Renovation of the Body in the Poetry of William Blake*. Ithaca, NY: Cornell University Press.

Galbraith, John Kenneth (1958) *The Affluent Society*. Boston: Houghton Mifflin.

Galbraith, John Kenneth (1973) *Economics and the Public Purpose*. Boston: Houghton Mifflin.

Gierke, Otto (1958) *Political Theories of the Middle Age*. Tran. with introduction by F.W. Maitland. Cambridge: Cambridge University Press.

Gilbert, Scott F. (1995) 'Resurrecting the body: has postmodernism had any effect on biology?', *Science in Context* 8 (4): 563–77.

Grene, Marjorie (1965) *Approaches to Philosophical Biology*. New York: Basic.

Griaule, Marcel (1965) *Conversations with Ogotommêli: An Introduction to Dogon Religious Ideas*. London: Oxford University Press.

Habermas, Jürgen (1975) *Legitimation Crisis*. Tran. Thomas McCarthy. Boston: Beacon.

Habermas, Jürgen (1984) *The Theory of Communicative Competence*. Boston: Beacon.

Hacker, Andrew (1982) 'Farewell to the family?', *The New York Review of Books*, March 18: 37–44.

Harris, Marvin (1977) *Cows, Pigs, Wars and Witches: The Riddles of Culture*. London: Collins.

Harris, Marvin (1978) *Cannibals and Kings*. London: Collins.

Harris, Marvin (1979) 'Cannibals and kings: an exchange', *The New York Review of Books*, June 28: 51–3.

Haraway, Donna J. (1991) *Simians, Cyborgs and Women: The Reinvention of Nature*. London: Routledge.

Haraway, Donna J. (1997) *Modest_Witness @ Second_Millenium Female Man © Meets_ OncoMouse™: Feminism and Technoscience*. New York: Routledge.

Hertz, Robert (1960) *Death and the Right Hand.* Tran. Rodney and Claudia Needham. Glencoe, IL: Free Press.

Hirschman, Albert O. (1977) *The Passions and the Interests: Political Arguments for Capitalism before its Triumph.* Princeton, NJ: Princeton University Press.

Holtzman, Neil A. (1989) *Proceed with Caution: Genetic Testing in the Recombinant DNA Era.* Baltimore, MD: Johns Hopkins University Press.

Horrobin, David F. (1977) *Medical Hubris: A Reply to Ivan Illich.* Montreal: Eden Press.

Hunt, Lynn (1992) *The Family Romance of the French Revolution.* Berkeley, CA: University of California Press.

Illich, Ivan (1975) *Medical Nemesis: The Expropriation of Health.* London: Calder & Boyars.

Illich, Ivan (1977) *Toward a History of Needs.* New York: Pantheon.

Illich, Ivan (1978) *The Cultural Crisis of Modern Medicine.* Ed. John Ehrenreich. New York: Monthly Review Press.

Illich, Ivan (1982) *Gender.* New York: Pantheon.

Kantorowicz, Ernst (1957) *The King's Two Bodies.* Princeton, NJ: Princeton University Press.

Lappé, Frances Moore (1975) *Diet for a Small Planet.* New York: Ballantine.

Lasch, Christopher (1980) 'Life in the therapeutic state', *The New York Review of Books,* June 12: 24–32.

Leach, Edmund (1964) 'Anthropological aspects of language: animal categories and verbal abuse', in Eric H. Lenneberg (ed.), *New Directions in the Study of Language.* Cambridge, MA: MIT Press.

Leach, Edmund (1967) 'Genesis as myth', in John Middleton (ed.), *Myth and Cosmos: Readings in Mythology and Symbolism.* Garden City, NY: Natural History Press, pp. 1–13.

Leach, Edmund (1970) *Claude Lévi-Strauss.* New York: Viking.

Leach, Gerald (1972) *The Biocrats: Implications of Medical Progress.* Harmondsworth: Penguin.

Lefebvre, Henri (1971) *Everyday Life in the Modern World.* Tran. Sacha Rabinovitch. London: Allen Lane.

Leiss, William (1978) 'Needs, exchanges and the fetishism of objects', *Canadian Journal of Political and Social Theory,* 2: 27–48.

Lévi-Strauss, Claude (1965) 'Le triangle culinaire', *L'Arc,* 26: 19–29.

Lévi-Strauss, Claude (1966) *The Savage Mind.* Chicago: University of Chicago Press. Lévi-Strauss, Claude (1970) *The Raw and the Cooked: Introduction to a Science of Mythology,* vol. 1. Tran. John and Doreen Weightman. New York: Harper & Row.

Levy, René (1976) 'Psychosomatic symptoms and women's protest: two types of reaction to structural strain in the family', *Journal of Health and Social Behavior,* 17: 122–34.

Lingis, Alphonso F. (1978) 'Savages' *Semiotext(e)* III/2.

Livy (1960) *The Earthly History of Rome,* Books I–IV of *The History of Rome from its Foundation.* Tran. Aubrey de Selincourt. Harmondsworth: Penguin.

Machiavelli, Niccolò (1980) *The Discourses of Niccolò Machiavelli.* Tran. with introduction and notes by Leslie J. Walker. London: Routledge & Kegan Paul.

MacRae, Donald G. (1975) 'The body and social metaphor', in *The Body as a Medium of Expression: An Anthology.* Ed. with an introduction by Jonathan Benthall and Ted Polhemus. New York: Dutton, pp. 59–73.

Mandeville, Bernard (1970) *The Fable of the Bees,* ed. Phillip Harth. Harmondsworth; Penguin Books.

Manning, Peter K. and Fabrega, Jr., Horacio (1973) 'The experience of self and body: health and illness in the Chiapas Highlands', in George Psathas (ed.), *Phenomenological Sociology: Issues and Applications.* New York: Wiley, pp. 251–301.

Marmorstein, Arthur (1937) *The Old Rabbinic Doctrine of God, II. Essays in Anthropomorphism.* Oxford: Oxford University Press.

Mauss, Marcel (1973) 'Techniques of the body', *Economy and Society,* 2: 70–88.

McIntosh, Mary (1978) 'The state and the oppression of women', in Annette Kuhn and Ann Marie Wolpe (eds), *Feminism and Materialism: Women and Modes of Production.* Boston: Routledge & Kegan Paul, pp. 254–89.

Melrose, Diane (1982) *Bitter Pills: Medicines and the Third World Poor.* Oxford: Oxfam.

Merleau-Ponty, Maurice (1962) *Phenomenology of Perception.* Tran. Colin Smith. London: Routledge & Kegan Paul.

Miller, Jonathan (1978) *The Body in Question.* London: Jonathan Cape.

Milunsky, Aubrey and Annas, George J. (eds) (1975 and 1980) *Genetics and the Law,* I and II. New York: Plenum Press.

Mitchell, Juliet (1966) 'Women: the longest revolution', *New Left Review,* (November-December): 11–37.

Montaigne, Michel (1965) *The Complete Essays of Montaigne.* Tran. Donald M. Frame. Stanford, CA: Stanford University Press.

Navarro, Vicente (1975) 'The industrialization of fetishism or the fetishism of industrialization: a critique of Ivan Illich', *Social Science and Medicine,* 9: 351–63.

Navarro, Vicente (1979) 'Social class, political power and the state: their implications in medicine,' in .J.W. Freiberg (ed.), *Critical Sociology: European Perspectives.* New York: Irvington, pp. 297–344.

Oakeshott, Michael (1967) *Rationalism in Politics and Other Essays.* London: Methuen.

Office of Technology Assessment (1988) *Mapping Our Genes, Genome Projects: How Big, How Fast?* Washington, DC: Office of Technology Assessment.

Olson, Maynard, Hood, Leroy, Cantor, Charles and Botstein, David (1989) 'A common language for physical mapping of the human genome', *Science,* 245 (September): 1434–5.

O'Neill, John (1970) *Perception, Expression and History.* Evanston, IL: Northwestern University Press.

O'Neill, John (1972) *Sociology as a Skin Trade: Essays towards a Reflexive Sociology.* New York: Harper & Row.

O'Neill, John (1973a) 'Embodiment and child development: a phenomenological approach', in Hans Peter Dreitzel (ed.), *Recent Sociology No. 5: Childhood and Socialization.* New York: Macmillan, pp. 76–86. Reprinted in Chris Jenks (ed.), *The Sociology of Childhood: Essential Readings.* London: Batsford.

O'Neill, John (1973b) 'On Simmel's "sociological apriorities"', in George Psathas (ed.), *Phenomenological Sociology: Issues and Applications.* New York: Wiley, pp. 91–106.

O'Neill, John (1974) *Making Sense Together: An Introduction to Wild Sociology.* New York: Harper & Row.

O'Neill, John (1975) 'Lecture visuelle de l'espace urbain', in *Colloque d'esthétique appliquée à la création du paysage urbain: Collection presenté par Michel Conan.* Paris: Copedith, pp. 235–47.

O'Neill, John (1976a) 'Critique and remembrance', in John O'Neill (ed.), *On Critical Theory.* New York: Seabury, pp. 1–11.

O'Neill, John (1976b) 'Time's body: Vico on the love of language and institution', in Giorgio Tagliacozza and Donald Phillip Verene (eds), *Giambattista Vico's Science of Humanity.* Baltimore, MD: Johns Hopkins University Press, pp. 333–9.

O'Neill, John (1982a) 'Defamilization and the feminization of law in early and late capitalism', *International Journal of Law and Psychiatry,* 5: 255–69.

O'Neill, John (1982b) 'Looking into the media: revelation and subversion', in Michael J. Hyde (ed.), *Communication Philosophy and the Technological Age.* Alabama: University of Alabama Press, pp. 73–97.

O'Neill, John (1982c) *For Marx against Althusser, and Other Essays.* Washington, DC: University Press of America.

O'Neill, John (1989) *The Communicative Body: Studies in Communicative Philosophy, Politics and Sociology.* Evanston, IL: Northwestern University Press.

O'Neill, John (1990) 'AIDS as a globalizing panic', *Theory, Culture and Society,* 2, 7, 2–3 (June): 329–42.

O'Neill, John (1993) 'McTopia: eating time', in Krishan Kumar and Stephen Bann (eds), *Utopias and Millennium.* London: Reaktion Books, pp. 129–37.

O'Neill, John (1995) *The Poverty of Postmodernism.* London: Routledge.

O'Neill, John (1996) *Hegel's Dialectic of Desire and Recognition: Texts and Commentary.* Albany, NY: State University of New York.

O'Neill, John (2002a) *Incorporating Cultural Theory: Maternity at the Millennium*. Albany, NY: State University of New York.

O'Neill, John (2002b) *Plato's Cave: Television and Its Discontents*. Cresskill, NJ: Hampton Press, Inc.

Packard, Vance (1959) *The Status Seekers*. New York.

Pateman, Carole (1988) *The Sexual Contact*. Cambridge: Polity Press.

Pateman, Carole (1989) *The Disorder of Women, Democracy, Feminism and Political Theory*. Cambridge: Polity Press.

Plato (1941) *The Republic*. Tran. F.M. Cornford. Oxford: Clarendon Press.

Plato (1957) *Cosmology: The 'Timaeus' of Plato*. Tran. with commentary by Francis Macdonald Cornford. New York: Liberal Arts Press.

Rabinow, Paul (1996) *Essays on the Anthropology of Reason*. Princeton, NJ: Princeton University Press.

Rank, Otto (1968) *Art and Artist: Creative Urge and Personality Development*. Tran. Charles Francis Atkinson. New York: Agathon Press.

Robinson, John A.T. (1952) *The Body: A Study in Pauline Theology*. London: SCM Press.

Rose, Nikolas (1999) *Powers of Freedom: Reforming Political Thought*. Cambridge: Cambridge University Press.

Rose, Nikolas (2001) 'The politics of life itself', *Theory, Culture and Society*, 18 (6): 1–30.

Rossi, Alice. S. (1973) 'Maternalism, sexuality and the new feminism', in Joseph Zubin and John Money (eds), *Contemporary Sexual Behaviour: Critical Issues in the 1970s*. Baltimore, MD: Johns Hopkins University Press.

Sahlins, Marshall (1976) *Culture and Practical Reason*. Chicago: University of Chicago Press.

Sahlins, Marshall (1978) 'Culture as protein and profit', *The New York Review of Books*, November 23: 45–53.

Sahlins, Marshall (1979) 'Cannibalism: an exchange', *The New York Review of Books*, March 22: 45–7.

Scarry, Elaine (1985) *The Body in Pain: The Making and Unmaking of the World*. New York: Oxford University Press.

Sennett, Richard, and Cobb, Jonathan (1973) *The Hidden Injuries of Class*. New York: Vintage.

Sheridan, Alan (1980) *Michel Foucault: The Will to Truth*. London: Tavistock.

Shilling, Chris (1993) *The Body and Social Theory*. London: Sage Publications.

Smith, Adam (1817) *Inquiry into the Nature and Causes of the Wealth of Nations*. Edinburgh.

Soler, Jean (1979) 'The dietary prohibitions of the Hebrews', *The New York Review of Books*, June 14: 24–30.

Stein, Gertrude (1934) *The Making of Americans*. New York: Harcourt, Brace.

Strathern, Marilyn (1992) *Reproducing the Future: Essays on Anthropology, Kinship and the New Reproductive Technologies*. New York: Routledge.

Tambiah, Stanley J. (1969) 'Animals are good to think and good to prohibit', *Ethnology*, 8: 424–59.

Taviss, Irene (1971) 'Problems in the social control of biomedical science and technology', in Everett Mendelsohn, Judith P. Swazey, and Irene Taviss (eds), *Human Aspects of Biomedical Innovation*. Cambridge, MA: Harvard University Press, pp. 3–45.

Thomas, Dylan (1952) *Collected Poems, 1934–1952*. London: Dent.

Titmuss, Richard M. (1971) *The Gift Relationship: From Human Blood to Social Policy*. New York: Vintage.

Trilling, Lionel (1950) *The Liberal Imagination: Essays on Literature and Society*. New York: Viking.

Turner, Bryan S. (1984) *The Body and Society: Explorations in Social Theory*. Oxford: Basil Blackwell.

Turner, Victor (1968) 'The word of the Dogon', *Social Science Information*, 7: 55–61.

Turner, Victor (1974) *Dramas, Fields, and Metaphors: Symbolic Action in Human Society*. Ithaca, NY: Cornell University Press.

Van Esterik, Penny (1989) *Beyond the Breast-Bottle: Controversy*. New Brunswick, NJ: Rutgers University Press.

Veblen, Thorstein (1925) *The Theory of the Leisure Class.* London: Allen & Unwin.

Vico, Giambattista ([1774] 1970) *The New Science of Giambattista Vico.* Tran. from the third edition by Thomas Goddard Bergin and Max Harold Fisch. Ithaca, NY: Cornell University Press.

Wagner, Roy (1986) *Symbols that Stand for Themselves.* Chicago: University of Chicago Press.

Wilson, Elizabeth (1977) *Women and the Welfare State.* London: Tavistock.

Wolstenholme, G.E.W. (1966) 'An old established procedure: the development of blood transfusion', in G.E.W. Wolstenholme and Maeve O'Connor (eds), *Ethics in Medical Progress, with Special Reference to Transplantation.* London: J. and A. Churchill, pp. 24–42.

Work in America: Report of a Special Task Force to the Secretary of Health, Education, and Welfare (1973) Cambridge, MA: MIT Press.

Index